THE ENVIRONMENTAL EFFECTS OF STABILIZATION AND STRUCTURAL ADJUSTMENT PROGRAMS: THE PHILIPPINES CASE

Wilfrido Cruz
Robert Repetto

WORLD RESOURCES INSTITUTE

September 1992

Kathleen Courrier
Publications Director

Brooks Clapp
Marketing Manager

Hyacinth Billings
Production Manager

World Bank Photo by Edwin G. Huffman
Cover Photo

Each World Resources Institute Report represents a timely, scientific treatment of a subject of public concern. WRI takes responsibility for choosing the study topics and guaranteeing its authors and researchers freedom of inquiry. It also solicits and responds to the guidance of advisory panels and expert reviewers. Unless otherwise stated, however, all the interpretation and findings set forth in WRI publications are those of the authors.

Contents

Acknowledgments

We are grateful to the many individuals who helped us during the course of this research. We especially thank Maria Concepción Cruz, who generously shared with us the results of her ongoing study on the determinants of population pressure and migration patterns in the Philippines. The Philippine upland migration data and the migration map in Part IV were based on her work. Cielito Habito, Director-General of the National Economic and Development Authority (NEDA), provided invaluable help in constructing the initial computable general equilibrium models and locating the data for our simulation experiments. Roy Boyd undertook the final CGE computations reported in Part V and prepared the methodological description in Appendix 5.2. Marian Delos Angeles, who is coordinating the Philippine government's own resource-accounting efforts, provided helpful comments on the forestry accounts in Part II.

We appreciate the encouragement given by key Philippine government officials, even though at the start they knew that the study was setting out to navigate uncharted waters. We especially thank Cayetano Paderanga, Jr., former Director-General of NEDA, and Fulgencio Factoran, Jr., former Secretary of the Department of Environment and Natural Resources (DENR). Ponciano Intal, Jr., President of the Philippine Institute for Development Studies, and Celso Roque, the former Undersecretary of DENR, were also very supportive.

Funding for the study was provided by the Rockefeller Foundation and the Netherlands Ministry for Development Cooperation.

Our special thanks go as well to WRI colleagues Paul Faeth, Owen Lynch, and Carrie Meyer, who provided helpful comments. We also received informal external comments and suggestions from Thomas Wiens, Klaus Schmidt-Hebbel, Cristina David, Rosario Manasan, William Hyde, and Gerald Nelson. External reviews were provided by Gardner Brown, Jr., David Nellor, Jeremy Warford, William J. Baumol, and Charles Howe. We appreciate their suggestions. Of course, we retain sole responsibility for the contents of this report.

Finally, we thank our research staff for putting up with numerous data requests and revisions. Fumiko Fukuoka helped construct the forestry-depreciation accounts as part of her master's thesis research, and prepared the methodological appendix on natural resource depreciation. Tony Zamparutti collected data for the structural adjustment and stabilization programs. Katy Perry and Rosemary McCloskey deserve thanks for their help with the wordprocessing, and Hyacinth Billings for her production coordination.

W.C.
R.R.

Foreword

The Earth Summit in Rio demonstrated worldwide support for the principle of sustainable economic development. Under the banner of sustainable development, governments, environmental activists, and development bankers now scrutinize the environmental impacts of such individual investment projects as roads and dams. Although the results of these assessments are often controversial and sometimes unsatisfactory, at least all participants agree that scrutinizing the possible environmental consequences of investment decisions is necessary and important.

Compared to decisions on individual investment projects, decisions on tax, credit, international trade, and other macroeconomic policies can have much more far-reaching and pervasive environmental consequences. By affecting the incentives of millions of firms and households, macroeconomic policies can either unleash or discourage resource exploitation and degradation. However, until now, the environmental consequences of macroeconomic policies have never been rigorously scrutinized. In fact, the models used by analysts in government and research institutes to project the results of macroeconomic policy decisions assume away all possible environmental consequences. They are simply outside the analysts' field of vision. Consequently, debates about the environmental sustainability of macroeconomic policies have been ill-informed and perfunctory.

With so many developing and formerly communist nations undergoing sweeping economic change, understanding the complex interconnections among macroeconomic policy change, structural economic change, poverty, population growth and environmental degradation is not an academic exercise but a pressing real-world necessity. In *The Environmental Effects of Stabilization and Structural Adjustment Programs: The Philippines Case*, Wilfrido Cruz, a former WRI associate and Robert Repetto, WRI vice president and senior economist, begin closing this knowledge gap. The authors examine the environmental implications of macroeconomic policies in the Philippines during the 1960s and 1970s, before the onset of the debt crisis in the early 1980s, and also the consequences of the ensuing stabilization and structural adjustment programs financed by the IMF and the World Bank. They find that macroeconomic policies in both periods had momentous, and little understood, environmental consequences.

In this study, a natural resource accounting methodology developed largely by WRI is applied to the Philippines to demonstrate that its development strategy drew down natural resource assets while it built up external financial obligations, markedly undermining the country's national balance sheet. Macroeconomic policies prior to the debt crisis provided few incentives to manage forests, soils, or fisheries for sustained productivity.

The analysis also shows how macroeconomic policies encouraged the rapid growth of relatively inefficient, pollution-prone processing industries, especially in the metropolitan Manila region, which consequently suffered severe environmental degradation. Although this process of overconcentration and degradation was observed as it occurred, little effort was made until too late to reverse the incentives that drove it.

Cruz and Repetto come to markedly different conclusions than previous observers about the environmental consequences of the stabilization policies designed to cope with the debt crisis. They find that the principal impact was not to force the Philippines to export its natural resources more rapidly to service the debt, as some have asserted. Because of the worldwide slump and domestic supply constraints, natural resource exports actually declined during the stabilization period. Rather, the principal impact was to send millions of unemployed and impoverished households as migrants into forested regions and onto marginal lands to seek a subsistence livelihood as shifting cultivators.

Based on their analysis, the authors conclude that structural adjustment policies, including trade liberalization and tariff reform, must be accompanied by other domestic policy changes to ensure sustainable use of natural resources. They point to options for the Philippines, such as reforms in resource taxation and land tenure, that could have forestalled much environmental damage, and they discuss alternative adjustment measures that could better have supported employment and eased the burden of poverty, thereby mitigating environmental pressures.

Policy-makers in development assistance agencies, international financial institutions, and developing countries can build on this report's analytical framework to design environmental considerations into structural adjustment and stabilization policies. It is to be hoped that the World Bank and the International Monetary Fund will develop and apply such new analytical approaches—and that environmental advocacy and watchdog organizations will elevate their scrutiny of national economic policies and structural reform programs.

The Environmental Effects of Stabilization and Structural Adjustment Programs: The Philippines Case extends and complements such recent WRI studies as *Accounts Overdue: Natural Resource Depreciation in Costa Rica, Paying the Farm Bill: U.S. Agricultural Policy and the Transition to Sustainable Agriculture, Wasting Assets: Natural Resources in the National Income Accounts,* and *The Forest for the Trees: Government Policies and the Misuse of Forest Resources.*

WRI would like to thank The Rockefeller Foundation and the Netherlands' Ministry for Development Cooperation, whose generous support made this study possible. We owe them a debt of gratitude for their support of WRI's work in natural resource accounting as well. To both, we express our deep appreciation.

James Gustave Speth
President
World Resources Institute

Part I. The Impact of Macroeconomic Policies on Natural Resources and the Environment

Two issues currently dominate the discussion of the Third World's economic prospects: the debt crisis and the continuing degradation of natural resources. These issues are linked. Many debt-burdened countries have suffered a decade of stagnant or falling living standards. Those unemployed or impoverished as a result have been driven to overexploit fragile, unproductive environments. Conversely, degraded natural resources also make sustained economic development more difficult.

Economic stagnation and unmanageable external debt have focused the attention of developing-country governments and donor agencies on macroeconomic policy reform—stabilization and structural adjustment programs. Stabilization programs are mainly intended to correct macroeconomic imbalances that are manifested in unmanageable fiscal or balance-of-payments deficits, or both. Stabilization programs usually reduce total expenditures significantly and shift resources to the production of internationally tradeable goods. They also include measures to refinance internal or external debt. Structural adjustment programs typically have the longer-term objective of reestablishing sustainable economic development and usually involve changes in exchange rate and trade policies, the size and structure of government expenditures, and the extent of government control over the economy.

Although the environmental effects of project lending by multilateral development banks has received much critical scrutiny, little attention has been paid until now to the possible environmental implications of structural adjustment and stabilization programs, or to macroeconomic policies in general. For example, the World Bank's most recent environmental progress report to its Board of Governors stated that "Adjustment lending has not, until recently, paid explicit attention to environmental issues." It also found that most country economic strategy studies done by the World Bank "discussed [environmental] issues only superficially."[1] These statements would apply even more emphatically to macroeconomic policy analysis carried out by the International Monetary Fund, the Interamerican Development Bank and other regional development banks, most bilateral development assistance agencies, and by developing-country governments.

Indeed, the macroeconomic accounting frameworks and analytical models used by such agencies generally assume away any possible environmental effects of macroeconomic policy instruments, such as taxes, interest rates, tariffs and exchange rates, and levels of public spending. Using such analytical tools, it is impossible even to examine whether particular policy changes would have beneficial, mixed, or adverse effects on natural resource use and environmental quality.

This study analyzes the implications for natural resource use of long-standing macroeconomic

1

strategies in the Philippines and of more recent economic stabilization and structural adjustment programs. It is one of the first attempts to construct and apply an analytical framework capable of assessing these linkages. The analysis focuses on the macroeconomic policies of the 1960s and 1970s that led to the Philippines debt crisis in the early 1980s. It also evaluates the environmental implications of structural adjustment and stabilization policies recommended as countermeasures to the debt crisis in the 1980s, and it identifies alternative approaches that address the urgency of economic recovery and resource conservation.

The report analyzes the effects of macroeconomic factors on natural resource use by examining the reallocation of economic activity along three axes: the first,—intertemporal—transferring resources between present and future generations, is discussed in Part II; the second,—intersectoral—reallocating resources among industries and affecting the mix of inputs used in production, is discussed in Part III; and the third,—interpersonal—altering the distribution of income and wealth among individuals and households, is discussed in Part IV. Part V presents the results of policy simulations using a computable general equilibrium model of the Philippines economy. These simulations compare the effects on natural resource use of prescribed structural adjustment policies with those of an alternative set of policy reforms.

A. A Summary of the Basic Findings

1. Intertemporal Effects: Resource Depletion and Foreign Debt

The first step in relating macroeconomic forces to natural resource use is measuring natural resources as economic assets in terms amenable to macroeconomic analysis. Natural resource accounting (Repetto et al. 1989) is a framework that measures resource depletion as an integral component of gross domestic capital formation, gross domestic product, and other important macroeconomic variables. In Part II, this framework is applied to establish the links between economic stagnation and ecological decline.

In essence, the Philippine development pattern was to deplete natural resource assets in order to finance current consumption and the acquisition of relatively unproductive industrial capital.

The analysis shows that, in essence, the Philippine development pattern was to deplete natural resource assets in order to finance current consumption and the acquisition of relatively unproductive industrial capital. In the Philippines, the shortfall in savings, the low returns on investments, and the continued increase in external indebtedness all shifted resources to current uses at the expense of future income. Macroeconomic policies depressed the returns private investors could obtain by holding or increasing natural resource assets, but inflated returns to industrial investments. These policies thus encouraged resource extraction and disinvestment in the primary production sector, which reduced sustainable yields from natural resources. Resource depreciation in just three sectors—forestry, soils, and coastal fisheries—averaged more than 4 percent of GDP from 1970–87 and 20 percent of gross investment. Under current national income-accounting methodologies, these asset losses are not recorded. Accordingly, conventional measures of gross and net capital formation substantially overstated the actual level of investment. (Figure 1.1).

Net disinvestment actually took place during the mid-1980s. While the annual resource depreciation rate exceeded 4 percent of GDP,

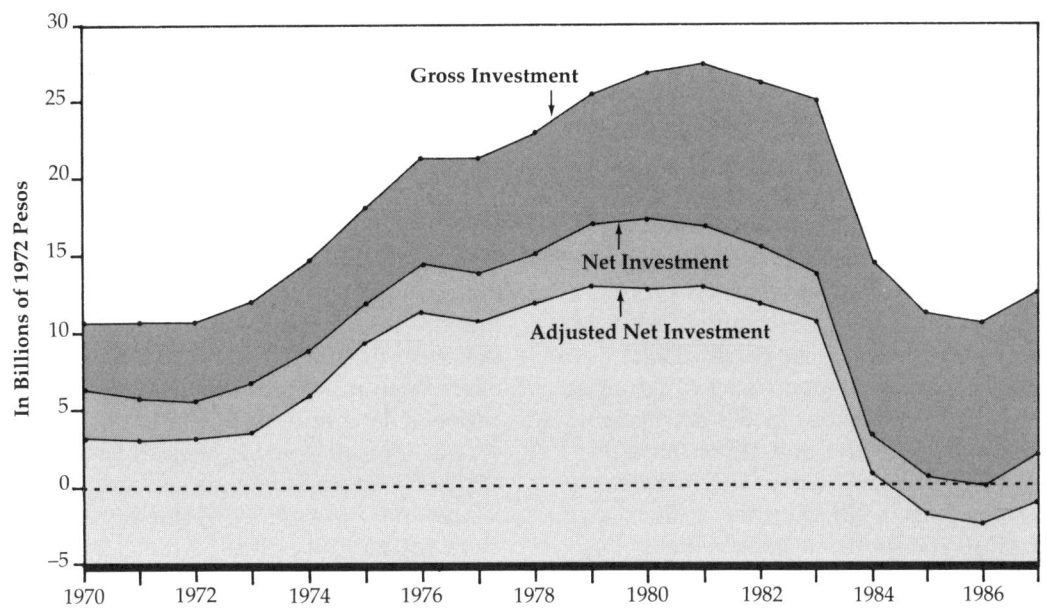

Figure 1.1 Investment Adjusted for Resource Depreciation

Note: Net Investment is Gross Investment less Capital Consumption Allowance. Adjusted Net Investment is Net Investment less forestry, soil and fishery resource depreciation from Part II. Investment data are from *Philippine Statistical Yearbook* (1989).

the current account deficit, indicating the rate of increase of external liabilities, averaged only 3.2 percent of GDP annually. Thus, the country's balance sheet was deteriorating more from resource depreciation than from foreign borrowing. Both stemmed from the intertemporal bias of macroeconomic policy, and both contributed to the ensuing economic crisis. But, unlike the highly publicized problem of external debt, unmeasured resource depreciation remained invisible.

Declining natural resources and growing external liabilities can be consistent with sustainable development for a time, if the process leads to new productive assets. However, infusions of capital to an excessively protected and inefficient industrial sector had low real rates

During the 70s and 80s the country's balance sheet was deteriorating more from resource depreciation than from foreign borrowing.

of economic return and did not provide an adequate alternative source of growth. Industry's incremental capital-output ratio (ICOR), a standard measure of the efficiency of investment, increased from 3.92 in 1970–74 to 6.37 from 1975–82. From 1983–88, the economy-wide ICOR continued to increase, averaging 9.48.[2]

2. Intersectoral Effects: Materials-Intensive and Energy-Intensive Industrial Growth, Spatial Concentration, and Increasing Pollution

Macroeconomic policies strongly affected the mix of inputs used in production and shifted resources among industrial sectors and geographic regions, as Part III shows. Tariff and exchange rate policies discouraged investment in the primary sector and promoted a progressive decapitalization of primary industries. Trade and exchange rate policies also kept manufactured consumer goods prices high and intermediate industrial input prices relatively low. As a result, from the mid-1950s through the mid-1980s, industry's use of intermediate inputs increased more rapidly than industrial output. Industry substituted intermediate inputs, including energy, for both capital and labor. In response to the distorted relative price incentives, Philippines industry became more materials-intensive. As a result, pollution from industrial emissions and consumer waste increased rapidly.

Fiscal incentives to industry reinforced this process by subsidizing most heavily such pollution-prone and energy-intensive sectors as pulp and paper, ferrous and non-ferrous metals, chemicals, and petroleum products. The economic crisis of the 1980s exacerbated the problems of industrial pollution because cuts in government spending undermined environmental regulation, waste collection, and treatment.

The heavy protection given to the final processing and assembly of consumer goods promoted industries closely tied to consumer markets and led industry to congregate in the metro Manila region. Government spending on transportation and other infrastructure was also focused primarily on the Manila area, and the dependence of industries on central government licenses, credit, and subsidies reinforced this geographical concentration. By the 1980s, two-thirds of all manufacturing establishments and 7 million households crowded the region, resulting in severe environmental degradation. Air and water quality monitoring over the past decade and a half indicate a progressively declining urban environment.

While energy policy in the Philippines allowed the increase in world petroleum prices to pass through into domestic energy prices, promoting energy conservation and the development of indigenous energy sources, this policy was blunted by macroeconomic policies that allowed the exchange rate to appreciate in the wake of both oil shocks. Exchange rate overvaluation, ranging from 14 to 24 percent between 1962 and 1988, artificially lowered the cost of imported oil, as well as that of other imported intermediate goods, and contributed to the energy-intensity of industrial development in the Philippines. An electricity pricing policy that kept rates well below marginal costs also contributed to this bias.

3. Interpersonal Effects: Unemployment, Poverty, and Population Pressure on Marginal Resources

Part IV traces the income and distributional effects of macroeconomic policies, examining the impact of unemployment and poverty on natural resource degradation. As this analysis shows, rapid population growth expanded the demand for agricultural staples and the supply of labor. In response, more acreage in the lowlands was first brought under cultivation; then, land-saving agricultural techniques using high-yielding seeds, irrigation, and chemicals were adopted. However, the transfer of labor out of agriculture lagged because industrial employment grew too slowly. As the momentum of the Green Revolution in lowland agriculture weakened, rural households looking for new livelihoods migrated into the uplands and into artisanal fisheries.

Macroeconomic policies intensified these trends. The trade regime, investment incentives, and credit policies all favored capital-intensive industries and retarded employment generation. They also penalized agriculture. Implicit taxes on agricultural incomes were as high as 20 percent, while government spending went to urban residents and to better-off agricultural areas. Under a credit rationing system, institutional finance went to industrialists and to larger farmers. Regressive taxation aggravated the income inequality resulting from these policies. At the same time, a highly concentrated distribution of both private agricultural holdings and use rights to public lands deprived most rural residents of access to these resources. Only the marginal resources in the public domain—forest lands, mangroves, and fisheries—remained available to a rapidly growing pool of landless workers.

As economic growth faltered in the 1980s and employment opportunities in lowland agriculture and in industry failed to expand, population pressure on these marginal resources increased. For example, migration to forest lands was already significant during the 1970s, though urban migration still dominated. With the economic crisis, net upland migration increased. It grew from 3.4 percent of the upland population during 1970–75, to 9.4 percent in 1975–80; during the economic crisis, it reached 14.5 percent. *(See Figure 1.2.)* Stabilization policies that sharply increased poverty and unemployment accelerated the degradation and deforestation of upper watersheds and the overexploitation of coastal fisheries and mangroves.

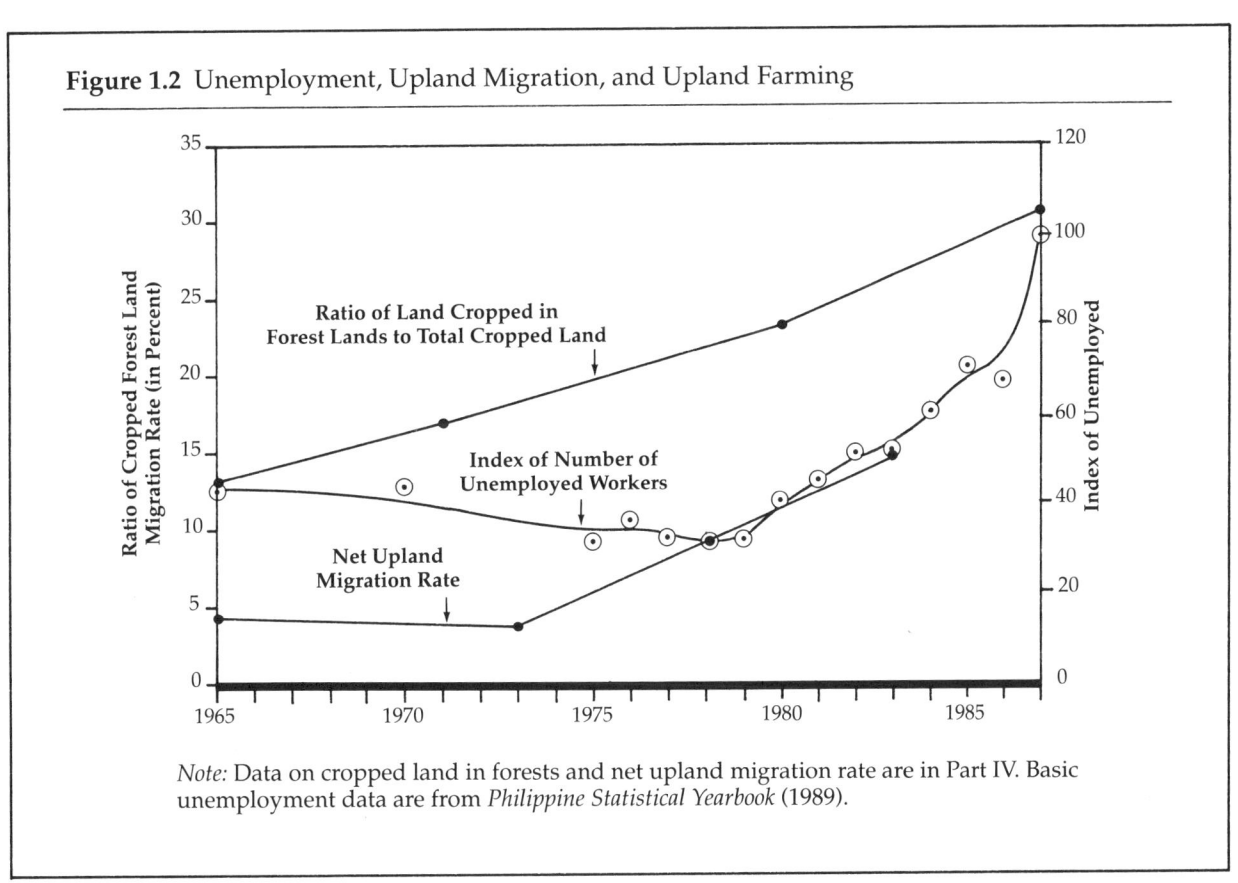

Figure 1.2 Unemployment, Upland Migration, and Upland Farming

Note: Data on cropped land in forests and net upland migration rate are in Part IV. Basic unemployment data are from *Philippine Statistical Yearbook* (1989).

B. Economic Crisis, Stabilization Policies, and Environmental Impacts

Part V describes the conditions leading to the Philippine debt crisis of the early 1980s and analyzes the stabilization and structural adjustment programs promoted by the International Monetary Fund and the World Bank. Despite the conventional view that the debt crisis intensified resource exploitation for export, the massive economic contraction associated with the collapse of world commodity prices and restrictive stabilization policies actually reduced domestic production of timber, minerals, and most other resource-based products.

This misplaced concern over the effect of the debt crisis on resource-based exports obscured its truly serious result—the increased exploitation of upland forests, coastal fisheries, and other marginal resources to which property rights are weak. The stabilization program was designed and executed with no regard for such environmental and social costs. The combined effects of the crisis and stabilization policies were massive unemployment and income decline. Real wages fell more than 20 percent between 1983 and 1985. As vastly increased numbers of workers migrated to the open access resources of the uplands and coastal areas, deforestation, soil erosion, the destruction of coastal habitats, and the depletion of fisheries increased.

C. The Impact of Alternative Structural Adjustment Policies on Natural Resources

The structural adjustment program during the early 1980s included standard World Bank prescriptions on trade liberalization, devaluation, export promotion, and energy conservation. It did not include adequate measures to deal with the environmental and resources pressures that would result from the structural adjustment package, even though the weakness of environmental and resource use controls in the Philippines at that time was well recognized.

The environmental consequences of macroeconomic policy changes can be fully analyzed only in a general equilibrium framework that adequately represents the effects of interrelated changes in relative prices and income levels on the demand for natural resources. For this purpose, a computable general equilibrium (CGE) model of the Philippines was constructed to highlight the effects of macroeconomic policy changes on production sectors such as logging, fishing, upland agriculture, mining, and energy supply that draw heavily on natural resources.

Most neoclassical macroeconomic models incorporate only capital and labor inputs into production, assuming away the importance of land and other natural resources. To redress this inadequacy, land inputs were incorporated into the CGE model, which allowed an assessment of land-use changes associated with alternative structural adjustment policies. Although the way the land input is analyzed in this model is admittedly crude,[3] it is nonetheless a first effort to incorporate natural resources into the analysis of structural adjustment programs.

The simulations demonstrate that the World Bank's structural adjustment reforms, if implemented fully, would have improved income and balance-of-payments conditions. Employment would also have grown, suggesting that migration to the uplands would have been reduced. However, because the proposed reforms stimulated economic activity without creating safeguards to prevent the overexploitation of natural resources, logging, over-fishing, mining, and erosion-prone upland agriculture would also have increased. The overall economic and environmental benefits of this adjustment program are uncertain, but certainly are inferior to those of an alternative structural adjustment package that includes institutional and policy reforms to achieve adequate control over industrial pollution and over the use of natural resources.

Alternative structural adjustment policies could have promoted growth, employment, and income distribution and, at the same time, reduced resource degradation. Analyses drawing on the CGE model results suggest that domestic resource mobilization based on resource rent taxes and environmental charges could reduce the balance-of-payment deficit, stimulate employment, and improve the distribution of income while reducing resource and environmental damage.[4] Also, measures to broaden access to agricultural lands could help control migration pressures on marginal resources. Had these opportunities for incorporating environmental considerations in structural reforms not been missed, policy changes could have helped put the Philippine economy on a more sustainable growth path.

Conclusions and Recommendations

Both structural adjustment and stabilization programs were implemented in the Philippines during the economic crisis of the early 1980s. Government imposed severe demand-reducing policies as part of stabilization programs supported by IMF standby arrangements. The subsequent economic contraction was so massive that the structural adjustment program was sidetracked. The crisis had severe environmental effects. Opportunities to ease the impact on labor and the poor were missed, and real wages fell sharply. Poverty and unemployment increased, triggering labor migration and overexploitation of marginal open-access resources.

Although the International Monetary Fund views its mandate primarily in terms of stabilizing short-term economic imbalances, the stabilization program it supported clearly had significant environmental consequences. Such consequences must be recognized if the environmental costs of future programs are to be reduced. The IMF, along with national macroeconomic policy authorities, must develop analytical methods that adequately predict the social and environmental implications of stabilization programs. Since the environmental costs arose mainly through the increase in poverty and underemployment, efforts to mitigate the social costs of stabilization programs in the Philippines could also have reduced environmental costs.

Environmental concerns were not adequately incorporated in the World Bank's structural adjustment program, either. Even if these reforms had not been held up by the economic contraction, simulation experiments suggest that adjustment policies would have intensified many of the detrimental environmental effects of the crisis. Structural adjustment programs that supported trade liberalization, industrial promotion, and energy conservation were formulated with limited regard for the environmental requirements of sustainable development.

The cornerstone of structural adjustment, trade liberalization, would have had desirable effects on income, the balance of payments, and energy conservation.[5] However, the same trade reforms would also have stimulated mining, logging, and erosion-prone upland agriculture, which all had severe, unregulated environmental costs. The record of industrial incentives reform was even worse. These incentives increased total output and employment marginally, but their balance-of-payments and income distribution effects were unfavorable and they encouraged more resource degradation and energy use.

The formulation of adjustment programs should incorporate as intrinsic and fundamental components, measures to strengthen control over resource depreciation, industrial pollution, and over-exploitation of open access resources. Without such measures, the environmental and overall economic implications of structural adjustment programs may be adverse. Fortunately, instruments for improving environmental and resource management while contributing to other adjustment objectives are available. For example, domestic resource mobilization, as well as environmental goals, can be served by re-structuring the tax system to strengthen rent and property taxation. Higher taxes on resource rents would reduce competition for lucrative concessions, capture resources for government programs (with some funds earmarked for resource management), and improve income distribution. Environmental charges or equivalent measures can also be used to limit the environmental effects of degradation-prone activities.

Structural adjustment could eliminate the bias against agricultural activities that are relatively benign environmentally. Such activities include labor-intensive foodcrop production in lowland rainfed areas, coconut growing, other plantation cropping, and agroforestry on sloping lands. Complementary measures to improve access to agricultural resources, either through traditional methods of land reform or indirectly through agricultural land taxes, would have had favorable economic, social, and environmental effects. Although these reforms have been discussed, they were not included in the adjustment program.

Indeed, not until 1985 did adjustment lending include conditions pertaining to the reform of trade and pricing disincentives to agricultural production. At that time, a sectoral adjustment loan sought to reduce import levies on agricultual inputs, eliminate agricultural marketing monopolies, and privatize the trading activities of government corporations. Had such reforms been incorporated into earlier adjustment programs, they could have significantly reduced the economic hardships imposed by the stabilization program on the rural poor and reduced the adjustment program's adverse environmental effects.

How can macroeconomic policy be made environmentally sensitive? The first hurdle to cross is methodological. Conventional macroeconomic models exclude by assumption the effects of macroeconomic changes on natural resource use and environmental conditions.

This study demonstrates that natural resource accounting is a useful empirical tool for analyzing long-term patterns of resource depreciation. Indeed, to assess the role of macroeconomic factors on the environment in developing countries, analysis must rest on an appropriate accounting framework.

Almost instinctively, many environmentalists, researchers, and officials of environment ministries, recognize the pivotal importance of constructing such accounts. In contrast, the official keepers of national accounts in the financial ministries and statistical offices of individual countries and in the international statistical community resist the demand to reform the inadequate national income accounting system. Some apparently believe that they have the luxury of time to wait for all the data and methodological refinements to become available everywhere before altering the standard framework. Yet, the existing accounting exercises show that natural resource depletion rates are so great that even partial estimates for just the principal sectors provide important insights into economic performance. Macroeconomic analyses based on an accounting framework that ignore this information almost inevitably lead to erroneous conclusions and faulty prescriptions.

A second hurdle is the lack of macroeconomic models, based on defensible accounting frameworks, that relate natural resource use and environmental impacts to macroeconomic policy changes. Until they are constructed, environmental objectives will not enter directly into macroeconomic programs. Unless the environmental costs of macroeconomic policies are made explicit, governments and international agencies will probably continue to adhere to myopic policies, at the expense of the majority of current and future households. Even environmental ministries, for all their site- and project-specific conservation activities, will generally consider national economic planning issues beyond their range of concern.

Environmental agencies should recognize that they also need to take positions on national economic policy since, as this study shows, macroeconomic policies and trends have important environmental implications. Similarly, environmental organizations need to focus on macroeconomic strategy, demographic change, and resource access issues.

Finally, the World Bank and the IMF, as two leading influences on the design of macroeconomic policy in the developing world, must actively promote new programs that simultaneously address structural adjustment and environmental needs. The analytical tools and the basic data needed to do this must be further developed and brought to bear on the increasing problems of the developing world, country by country. Oversight groups should demand that the environmental consequences of macroeconomic reforms be analyzed and that environmental goals be explicitly integrated in their design and implementation.

Part II. Unsustainable Growth and Ecological Decline

A. Development, Depletion, and Debt

The Philippines' national income accounts before the debt crisis would reveal little obvious cause for concern. Although GNP growth in the 1970s was somewhat below the high rates achieved during the 1950s, it still averaged well over 6 percent per year over the decade. (*See Table 2.1.*) However, had national balance sheets been available, they would have shown a dangerous deterioration. Growth was maintained during the decade by building up external indebtedness and drawing down important domestic assets, especially natural resources. Like a highly leveraged business, the Philippines economy was increasingly vulnerable to external shocks and internal structural flaws.

Savings rates averaged about 19 percent of GNP from 1960–74 while gross investment rates were about 20 percent of GNP (World Bank 1976). During this period, government expanded its role in the economy, investing not only in infrastructure but also in trading and processing activities traditionally reserved for the private sector. International financial institutions and bilateral donor agencies supported the growth of government and of state enterprises.[6] For example, one of the World Bank's key programs in the mid-1970s was to promote government investment and domestic resource mobilization (World Bank 1976). By the late 1970s, conventionally measured investment rates had grown to about 30 percent of GNP but savings rates were only 23 to 25 percent of GDP.

The gap between domestic savings and investment was filled by external borrowing. Most of the debt inflow during the 1970s financed investment in government projects or private investments guaranteed by government banks. These investments were "ill-conceived, over-priced, or proved unprofitable in a rapidly changing international environment."[7]

While foreign borrowing financed unproductive capital projects, the depletion of productive natural resources was ignored by the international donor community. For example, forestry programs promoted wood-processing industries, while the logging boom that started in the late 1960s and continued into the 1970s reduced the land under forests from 34 percent of total area in the mid-1960s to 21 percent in 1987. Fisheries programs financed more efficient fishing and processing equipment without serious regard for sustainable fisheries management. Fishery and mangrove exploitation intensified in the 1970s, leading to declining productivity in the early 1980s. Mining, especially of copper, expanded so rapidly that by the end of the 1970s the Philippines was one of the world's leading copper exporters.

The Philippines economy was unable to develop a buoyant, rapidly expanding industrial sector, as other East Asian countries have

Table 2-1. Average Annual Growth Rate of GDP by Major Sectors, 1951—1989

Sectors	1951–60	1961–70	1971–75	1976–80	1981–85	1986–89
Agriculture	5.3	4.0	4.3	5.3	2.1	2.3
Industry	7.1	5.3	8.4	7.5	−2.6	5.4
Manufacturing	9.8	5.6	7.0	6.0	−1.3	5.8
Services	7.3	4.9	5.7	5.8	−0.3	5.7
GDP	6.5	4.8	6.2	6.2	−0.5	4.6

Sources:

1. 1951–60 data from NEDA (1978). *The National Income Accounts*, CY 1946—1975, Philippine National Income Series No. 5. Manila: NEPA.

2. 1961–70 estimates from Pante and Medalla (1990). The national accounts up to 1967 and from 1967 to the present were based on different methodologies, which required adjustments to make them comparable.

3. 1971–88 data from 1989 *Philippine Statistical Yearbook*; 1989 preliminary data from Pante and Medalla (1990).

done. The import-substitution strategy of the 1950s had lost momentum by the end of the 1960s. To save foreign exchange and to promote industrial growth, imports of manufactured consumer goods had been limited by quantitative restrictions from the 1950s to the 1970s and, after 1962, by high tariffs. The Central Bank classified consumer goods as ''nonessential'' imports and capital goods and imported intermediate goods as ''essential.'' Restrictions on imports of ''non-essentials'' made it more profitable in the Philippines to produce ''non-essential'' consumer goods than ''essential'' commodities. But, as opportunities in consumer goods industries were filled, manufacturing growth rates declined substantially.

Instead of promoting industries with clear cost advantages, the industrial promotion system and trade policies diverted domestic resources to high-cost protected industries. As one indication, the incremental capital-output ratio (ICOR) in industry increased from 3.9 in 1970–74 to 6.37 from 1975–82. Sectoral breakdowns cannot be computed for more recent years, but the economy-wide ICOR averaged 9.48 from 1983–88.[8]

Recurring Trade Deficits

Highly protected industries were not only dependent on foreign exchange to finance imported intermediate inputs; they also had little capacity to export.[9] From 1968–74, there was an enormous increase of industrial raw materials and intermediate input imports, and intermediate industrial inputs replaced finished consumer goods as the largest component of the import bill.[10] But on the eve of the first oil shock, the Philippines was still heavily dependent on traditional primary commodity exports for foreign exchange earnings. These characteristics made the economy vulnerable to the increase in oil prices and the decline in other commodity prices that characterized the oil crises. *(See Table 2.2.)* The Philippines' terms of trade declined by roughly 50 percent from the late 1960s to the mid-1980s.

Table 2-2. Resource and Non-Traditional Exports in Philippine Trade, 1960–87 (F.O.B. value, in million U.S. dollars)

	1960	1970	1975	1980	1981	1982	1983	1984	1985	1986	1987
1. Total Philippine Exports	535	1,142	2,294	5,788	5,720	5,021	5,005	5,391	4,629	4,842	5,720
2. Forestry and Mineral Products	132	508	574	1,285	1,138	858	744	561	442	491	512
Percent share of (1)	24.7	44.5	25.0	22.2	19.9	17.1	14.9	10.4	9.5	10.1	9.0
Forest Products	95	301	260	468	469	362	331	323	246	251	306.3
Logs	85	243	167	92	76	78	74	88	39	26	0.3
Lumber	7	13	27	181	126	124	149	107	90	103	154
Plywood	2	20	21	111	111	67	76	56	51	56	67
Others	1	25	45	84	156	93	32	72	66	66	85
Mineral Products	37	207	314	817	669	496	413	238	196	240	206
Copper Concentrates	30	185	212	545	429	312	249	115	84	90	109
Gold	—	—	76	239	215	169	154	104	100	140	90
Iron Ore and Concentrates	—	13	13	0	0	0	0	0	0	0	0
Chromite Ore	5	9	13	33	25	15	10	19	12	10	7
Others	2	17	18	214	89	36	27	28	47	27	18
3. Ten Principal Exports	477	868	1,619	2,635	2,315	1,672	1,730	1,646	1,125	1,068	1,122
Percent share of (1)	89.2	76.0	70.6	45.5	40.5	33.3	34.6	30.5	24.3	22.1	19.6
Logs and Lumber Exports	92	256	194	273	202	202	223	194	130	130	155
Percent share of (3)	19.3	29.5	12.0	10.4	8.7	12.1	12.9	11.8	11.6	12.2	13.8
Gold and Copper Exports	30	185	288	784	645	481	403	219	184	230	200
Percent share of (3)	6.3	21.3	17.8	29.8	27.9	28.8	23.3	13.3	16.4	21.5	17.8
4. Non-Traditional Manufactures	—	95	374	2,107	2,572	2,461	2,537	2,991	2,564	2,685	3,604
Percent share of (1)	—	8.3	16.3	36.4	45.0	49.0	50.7	55.5	55.4	55.5	63.0

Even earlier, Philippine economic development was hampered by recurring balance-of-payment problems. During the late 1960s, current account deficits grew to 3.7 percent of GDP. The government was forced to devalue the peso early in 1970 and to enact a non-traditional export incentive program later that year, raising the effective exchange rate for untraditional exports by 57 percent. (Lamberte et al., 1989) Effective exchange rates continued to improve for exporters through 1978, except for the massive interruption when imported energy price increased in 1974. *(See Table 2.3.)* In response, manufactured exports, principally garments, semiconductors, and handicrafts, expanded by more than 30 percent per year after 1974, even though world commodity prices declined.

However, the structure of incentives continued to penalize agriculture and exports in the mid-1970s and even into the mid-1980s.

Table 2-3. Indicators of External Sector, 1967–89

Year	Index of Terms of Trade ('72 = 100)	Current Account Balance (% of GNP)	Peso-Dollar Exchange	Real Effective Exchange Rate Index ('72 = 100)
1967–71	120	−0.7	n.a.	n.a.
1972	100	0.1	6.67	100.00
1973	113	5.0	6.76	105.01
1974	115	−1.2	6.79	87.88
1975	88	−5.6	7.25	96.79
1976	78	−5.8	7.44	100.43
1977	71	−3.6	7.40	102.94
1978	79	−4.9	7.37	110.60
1979	87	−5.4	7.38	98.41
1980	69	−5.4	7.51	92.51
1981	58	−6.2	7.90	90.21
1982	59	−6.8	8.54	87.30
1983	55	−7.4	11.11	107.49
1984	59	−2.3	16.70	105.04
1985	61	−1.7	18.61	92.80
1986	67	−0.7	20.39	117.64
1987	64	−3.0	20.57	124.76
1988	85	−2.8	21.09	128.67
1989	n.a.	n.a.	21.74	122.11

Sources: Philippine Statistical Yearbook (various issues), Alburo and Shepherd (1991), Remolona et al. (1986), Pante and Medalla (1989).

(See Table 2.4.) Effective rates of protection in 1974 averaged only 4 percent for exported commodities, compared to 61 percent for non-exportables. By the end of the 1970s, as the real exchange rate appreciated again, exports stagnated despite surging oil import costs. Clearly, part of the problem was the worsening terms of trade associated with the second oil price shock (in 1979) and the world recession in the early 1980s—factors out of the control of macroeconomic managers. However, the government's exchange rate policy allowed effective exchange rates to deteriorate for exporters from 1978–82. *(See Table 2.3.)*

Natural resource export earnings also dropped during the 1980s. *(See Table 2.2.)* The

By the mid-1970s much of the Philippines' prime old-growth tropical hardwood stock had been cut, and the timber boom was over.

decline in resource exports can be attributed partly to falling commodity prices, especially in the minerals industry: copper prices, for example, fell from about $3 per pound in the 1970s to about $.60 per pound in the early 1980s. Log exports declined primarily as the result of supply

Table 2-4. Average Effective Protection Rate by Major Industry Group (%), 1974, 1985, and 1988			
Industry Group	**1974**	**1985**	**1988**
1. Agriculture and Primary	9	6.6	1.4
2. Manufacturing	44	38.0	33.1
3. Exports	4	−5.8	−3.2
4. Non-exportable	61	–	–
—import-competing	37	54.5	43.7
—not import-competing	148	–	–
Overall Average	36	27.3	22.5

Sources: Tan (1979) for 1974 and Medalla (1990) for 1985 and 1988.

constraints. More than two decades of intensive exploitation had reduced forested land from more than one third of total land area in the late 1960s to less than one fourth by the mid-1980s. (DENR, 1989a) By the mid-1970s much of the prime old-growth tropical hardwood stock had been cut, and the timber boom was over. Despite the devaluation, improved export incentives in the early 1970s, and increasing timber prices throughout the 1970s, harvest and export volume fell continuously during the decade.[11]

Growing External Debts

The declining terms of trade and inadequate export performance in the late 1970s led to a growing trade deficit financed through external borrowing. The current account deficit increased to 5.6 percent of GDP after the first oil crisis and reached 7.8 percent of GDP in the world recession following the second oil crisis. Up to the mid-1960s, the deficit was financed from foreign exchange reserves (Alburo and Shepherd 1991). Afterward, it was financed through increased external borrowing. External debt as a proportion of GDP remained below 10 percent for most of the 1950s and the early 1960s, but after 1967 consistently increased, averaging 28 percent during the 1970s and 64 percent from 1980 to 1988. The country's debt burden was increasing substantially, and a crisis became inevitable once adverse external conditions cut off new foreign lending in the early 1980s. Foreign borrowing allowed the government to continue running budget deficits and to maintain spending levels. When this strategy collapsed in the early 1980s, both public and private investment fell by half relative to the level of GDP. *(See Table 2.5.)*

Many of the investments that foreign borrowing had financed were guaranteed by government and were part of the Marcos administration's system of parcelling out favors to political and economic allies. (De Dios, 1984) These investments mostly ended up as public liabilities when they proved unprofitable. Although such wasteful and inefficient projects were termed "investment," they also shifted income toward the present at the expense of the future.

Domestic savings lagged behind investment throughout the 60s, 70s, and 80s. Savings rates remained below 20 percent for most of the mid-1960s to mid-1970s. Government saving performance relative to its investment rate was even worse because of its dismal taxation record. Total tax revenues traditionally comprised only about 10 percent of GDP, in contrast to most countries in the region that had ratios of 15 percent or more. Increased external indebtedness filled the gap between growing investment and current expenditures and limited domestic resource mobilization.

Table 2-5. Domestic Resource Gap and Foreign Borrowing, 1978–1985

Domestic Resource Gap	1978	1979	1980	1981	1982	1983	1984	1985
Investment (% of GNP)	29.0	31.0	30.7	30.7	28.8	27.1	19.2	16.2
Private	22.4	25.0	22.8	22.0	21.8	19.4	14.6	12.6
Public	6.6	6.0	7.9	8.7	7.0	7.7	4.6	3.6
Savings (% of GNP)	23.7	25.6	25.0	24.7	20.3	18.9	16.0	15.6
Private	20.2	21.0	20.1	21.1	19.1	15.4	15.0	14.6
Public	3.5	4.6	4.9	3.6	1.2	3.5	1.0	1.0
Public Sector Deficit (% of GNP)	−3.1	−1.4	−3.0	−5.1	−5.8	−4.2	−3.0	−2.6
Investment— Savings Gap (% of GNP)	−5.3	−5.4	−5.7	−6.0	−8.5	−8.2	−2.6	−0.6
Foreign Borrowing								
External Debt (% of GDP)	34.0	33.0	36.0	54.4	61.8	70.8	75.6	82.0
Debt Service (% of export of goods and services)	20.8	20.3	18.7	33.5	42.4	36.3	33.3	32.5

Source: World Bank (1987), *Philippine Statistical Yearbook,* Various Issues.

In the 1970s a pattern of intertemporal resource use emerged that maintained current consumption at the expense of the future. It was characterized by poor government revenue performance, limited savings, and inefficient investments.

In short, in the 1970s a pattern of intertemporal resource use emerged that maintained current consumption at the expense of the future. It was characterized by poor government revenue performance, limited savings,

and inefficient investments. The economic crisis magnified this fiscal imbalance. As a share of GNP, total consumption did not decline during the crisis. From about 76 percent at the end of the 1970s, it instead increased to 84 percent in 1984 and close to 89 percent in 1985. (World Bank, 1987) Saving and investment all but collapsed, making recovery all the more difficult.

B. Ecological Decline and Resource Depreciation

Mounting external liabilities were open evidence of the government's willingness to maintain current expenditures by mortgaging the future. Less obvious but no less important was the depreciation of natural resource assets.

Commercial forests, agricultural soils, and fisheries had been depleted. Overexploitation also degraded resources. For example, even if intensive harvesting of tropical fish stocks had not reduced fishery biomass substantially, it would probably have degraded the fishery's economic value by increasing the proportion of less preferred species and juveniles as a proportion of total biomass. Both depletion and degradation reduce a resource's potential long-term yield in income and productive employment.

Natural resource accounting provides a macroeconomic framework for evaluating ecological decline. The national income accounts include a capital consumption allowance representing the value of the reproducible capital used up in producing the economy's annual output of goods and services. This capital consumption allowance permits a realistic assessment of net capital formation and net value added, and links a country's national income and balance sheet accounts. However, the accounts do not treat the depletion and degradation of natural resources in an analogous way, though in many countries a substantial proportion of annual production depends directly on natural resource exploitation. Ignoring natural resource depreciation blurs the distinction between activities that generate income and those that consume assets. For example, widespread deforestation may lead to large timber exports, but if no adjustment to the national accounts is made for the forest stock that will no longer be available for future exploitation, the country's income will be overestimated. Such a country could be losing most of its natural endowments, but the national accounts would indicate only an improvement in economic welfare. (Repetto et al., 1989). Natural resource accounting resolves the inconsistency by treating natural resources as part of the capital stock. Depreciation or enhancement of natural resource stocks can then be measured and analyzed like any other component of domestic capital formation.[12]

In the Philippines, there was net depreciation of forests, soils, and fisheries throughout the

period under review. *(See Table 2.6.)* For these three key sectors, the results indicate a general pattern of ecological decline and capital consumption. Over the 12 years preceding the Philippines' debt crisis, asset loss in just these three resources together averaged over 4 percent of GDP each year. By contrast, the annual current account deficit, indicating the rate at which external liabilities were building, averaged only 3.2 percent of GDP per year. The Philippines' national balance sheet was literally eroding, and at a much faster rate from natural resource deterioration than from the more publicized foreign borrowing. Both reflected the intertemporal bias of the government's macroeconomic policy. Both contributed to the ensuing economic crisis. The costs of servicing the foreign debt became increasingly heavy. The loss of natural resource assets also cost the economy dearly in output, exports, employment, and income.

Forestry Resources

Deforestation is perhaps the most costly form of resource depreciation in the Philippines. Actual forest cover declined from 34 percent to 21 percent during the last two decades.[13] A recent government-sponsored study concludes that forest depletion has been much faster than previously estimated. *(See Table 2.7.)* The Bureau of Forestry Development (1985) reported that deforestation from 1970 to 1985 totalled about 85,000 hectares per year. The Food and Agriculture Organization estimated a deforestation rate of 95,000 ha/yr for the same

Table 2-6. GDP Adjusted for Timber, Soil, and Fishery Depreciation, 1970–1987
(in million 1972 pesos)

	(1)				(2)	(3)	(4)
	Natural Resource Depreciation				Gross Domestic Product	"Net Domestic Product"	Resource Depreciation as % of GDP
	Timber	Upland Agric. Soil	Coastal Fishery	All Sectors			
1970	−2508	−139	−234	−2881	51014	48133	5.65
1971	−2476	−151	−234	−2861	53672	50811	5.33
1972	−2119	−163	−234	−2516	56464	53948	4.46
1973	−2577	−176	−234	−2987	60202	57215	4.96
1974	−2858	−188	−234	−3280	64187	60908	5.11
1975	−2599	−200	−234	−3033	68437	65404	4.43
1976	−2435	−212	−234	−2881	73922	71041	3.90
1977	−2824	−224	−234	−3282	78467	75185	4.18
1978	−2628	−236	−234	−3098	82784	79686	3.74
1979	−3341	−249	−234	−3824	87962	84138	4.35
1980	−4217	−261	−234	−4712	92568	87856	5.09
1981	−3427	−273	−234	−3934	96207	92273	4.09
1982	−2502	−285	−234	−3021	98999	95978	3.05
1983	−2596	−297	−234	−3127	99921	96794	3.13
1984	−2296	−309	−234	−2839	93927	91088	3.02
1985	−2422	−322	0	−2744	89904	87160	3.05
1986	−2369	−334	0	−2703	91287	88584	2.96
1987	−2649	−346	0	−2995	95948	92953	3.12

Note: Sectoral resource depreciation estimates are derived in the Section II.B. GDP data are from the *Philippine Statistical Yearbook*, various years.

period (FAO, 1983). Current estimates, however, suggest that between the late 1960s and the late 1980s, some 179,000 hectares per year were deforested. Dipterocarp forests (the most commercially valuable forest type) have been felled at about 176,000 hectares per year; 53 percent of remaining dipterocarp stands have already been logged over. 48 percent of remaining old-growth dipterocarp stands are in areas where slopes are over 50 percent. What forest is left has also been degraded (DENR Forestry Masterplan, 1989).

Timber resource accounts from 1970 to 1987 estimate depletion from conversion, logging,

and fire damage.[14] (See Table 2.8.) Increases in the timber stock from growth in secondary forests and reforestation are small compared to total depletion. So, timber stocks have declined throughout the period, from about 45 million cubic meters in the early 1970s to about 32 million cubic meters in the late 1980s. The value of the net annual loss in timber stock ranged from $182 million in 1970 to a peak of $1,618 million in 1980. From 1970 to 1987, timber resource depreciation amounted to 2 to 5 percent of GDP per year, averaging 3.3 percent. (See Table 2.9.) This asset loss alone exceeds the average annual increase in external indebtedness over the same period.

Table 2-7. Philippine Land Classification and Trends in Forest Cover

	First Inventory (1964–69)		Second Inventory (1984–87)		Annual Conversion (000 Has.)
	(000 Has.)	(% of total land area)	(000 Has.)	(% of total land area)	
Natural Forest Cover					
Dipterocarp	8096.00	27.00	4330.00	14.40	176.00
Pine	443.00	1.50	243.00	0.80	
Mangroves	249.00	0.80	136.00	0.50	
Mossy/Submarginal	1439.00	4.80	1603.00	5.30	
All Forest	10227.00	34.10	6313.00	21.00	179.00
Land Classification					
Official Forestland	8543.00	28.50	15011.00	50.00	
Alienable & Disposable	12572.00	41.90	14108.00	47.00	
Unclassified	8885.00	29.60	881.00	2.90	

Notes:
1. Data from DENR, RP-German Forest Resources Inventory, 1987 for various regions, as reported in Delos Angeles & Lasmarias, 1990. Annual conversion rate in the last column cannot be computed directly from columns one and three because the inventories were based on regional data for various years.
2. Data on land classification based on 1970 (for first inventory period) and 1987 (for second inventory period).

Soil and Watershed Resources

Upland soil resources and watershed systems have also been depreciating. Deforesting and converting steeply sloped lands into upland farms or pastures causes soil erosion. Erosion reduces the topsoil's organic matter and its waterholding capacity and so reduces its productive value in all subsequent cropping periods. The economic measure of soil depreciation is the capitalized value of this stream of losses in yields and income. In the aggregate, estimated soil depreciation losses ranged from 139 to 346 million pesos annually between 1970 and 1987, averaging 242 million pesos in 1972 prices.

Estimates for several large watersheds show that annual soil erosion from steeply sloped lands with substantial rainfall is only about 1 to 2 tons per hectare under forest cover but increases to 122 to 210 tons per hectare for newly established pastures and 11 to 178 tons per hectare for diversified crops (David, 1988). A study of the 400,000-hectare Magat watershed found that erosion averaged 50 tons per hectare per year for all land uses but exceeded 100 tons per hectare for open grasslands (David, 1988). In the absence of adequate data on losses in yields and net farm income due to erosion, the cost of soil erosion in the Magat watershed was measured as the cost of replacing lost nutrients (NPK) with fertilizers. This averages about $50 annually per hectare of land converted from forests to upland crops, 10 to 20 percent of the expected gross returns. (W. Cruz et al., 1988; World Bank, 1989b)

Table 2-8. Forestry Resource Depreciation, 1970–1987

	1970	1971	1972	1973	1974	1975	1976
I. PHYSICAL ACCOUNTS (million cubic meters)							
Opening Stock	1550.6	1505.6	1461.2	1420.8	1376.8	1333.3	1288.0
Additions							
Growth	4.2	4.2	4.2	4.2	4.2	4.2	4.2
Reforestation							0.4
Reductions							
Harvesting	11.0	10.7	8.4	10.5	10.2	11.2	8.7
Deforestation	29.0	29.0	29.0	29.0	29.0	29.0	29.0
Logging Damage	8.8	8.5	6.7	8.4	8.2	8.9	6.9
Fire Damage	0.4	0.4	0.4	0.4	0.4	0.4	0.4
Net Change	−45.0	−44.4	−40.4	−44.0	−43.5	−45.3	−40.4
Closing Stock	1505.6	1461.2	1420.8	1376.8	1333.3	1288.0	1247.6
II. UNIT VALUES (US$ per cubic meter)							
FOB Export Price	26.0	26.0	25.0	39.0	46.0	36.0	58.0
Costs	13.0	13.0	12.0	18.7	22.1	17.3	27.8
Primary Rent	14.0	13.0	13.0	20.3	23.9	18.7	30.2
Secondary Rent	6.5	6.5	6.5	10.1	12.0	9.4	15.1
III. MONETARY ACCOUNTS (US$ millions)							
Opening Stock		17028.3	16430.9	15884.7	23872.9	27107.8	20253.0
Additions							
Growth	27.3	27.3	27.3	35.0	46.5	44.9	51.4
Reforestation							
Reductions							
Harvesting	143.1	138.8	109.5	173.9	225.2	237.9	211.4
Deforestation	188.8	188.8	188.8	241.6	320.9	309.6	354.9
Logging Damage	57.3	55.5	43.8	69.6	90.1	95.2	84.6
Fire Damage	2.4	2.4	2.4	3.1	4.1	3.9	4.5
Net Change	−364.2	−358.2	−317.1	−453.1	−593.8	−601.8	−603.9
Revaluation		−239.2	−229.1	8441.3	3828.6	−6253.0	11770.1
Closing Stock	17028.3	16430.9	15884.7	23872.9	27107.8	20253.0	31419.2

Table 2-8. (Continued)

1977	1978	1979	1980	1981	1982	1983	1984	1985	1986	1987
1247.6	1209.1	1172.1	1136.0	1099.7	1065.7	1033.3	997.2	965.9	934.6	903.8
4.2	4.2	4.2	4.2	4.2	4.2	4.2	4.2	4.2	4.2	4.2
0.9	1.1	1.1	0.8	1.0	1.1	1.6	0.7	0.4	0.3	0.4
7.9	7.2	6.6	6.4	5.4	4.6	4.5	3.9	3.6	3.4	4.1
29.0	29.0	29.0	29.0	29.0	29.0	29.0	29.0	29.0	29.0	29.0
6.3	5.7	5.3	5.1	4.3	3.7	3.6	3.1	2.9	2.7	3.3
0.4	0.4	0.4	0.8	0.5	0.3	4.9	0.1	0.5	0.2	0.2
−38.5	−37.0	−36.1	−36.3	−34.1	−32.3	−36.2	−31.2	−31.3	−30.9	−32.1
1209.1	1172.1	1136.0	1099.7	1065.7	1033.3	997.2	965.9	934.6	903.8	871.7
65.0	66.0	116.0	129.0	108.0	104.0	94.0	104.0	90.0	90.0	112.0
31.2	31.7	47.0	49.0	51.0	54.0	59.0	49.9	43.2	43.2	53.8
33.8	34.3	69.0	80.0	57.0	50.0	35.0	54.1	46.8	46.8	58.2
16.9	17.2	34.5	40.0	28.5	25.0	17.5	27.0	23.4	23.4	29.1
31419.2	33920.0	32985.4	63492.0	70383.6	47986.3	40298.9	26698.8	39178.3	32148.5	30241.4
67.3	71.7	108.7	156.8	144.2	112.6	89.4	93.7	106.2	98.5	110.5
251.7	244.2	341.0	474.6	371.3	245.6	190.0	172.4	180.1	160.5	217.4
464.3	494.6	750.1	1081.7	994.6	776.8	617.1	646.7	732.4	679.5	762.6
100.7	97.7	136.4	189.8	148.5	98.2	76.0	68.9	72.0	64.2	87.0
5.9	6.3	9.6	28.1	17.6	8.9	103.4	2.9	12.2	4.1	5.8
−755.3	−771.1	−1128.3	−1617.5	−1387.9	−1017.0	−897.0	−797.2	−890.5	−809.9	−962.3
3256.2	−163.5	31634.9	8509.1	−21009.4	−6670.5	−12703.1	13276.8	−6139.3	−1097.2	6002.5
33920.0	32985.4	63492.0	70383.6	47986.3	40298.9	26698.8	39178.3	32148.5	30241.4	35281.6

Table 2-9. Forestry Depreciation Incorporated in National Accounts
(million 1972 pesos)

	(1) Forestry Depreciation (current $ million)	(2) Export Exchange Rate (P/US$)	(3) Loss in Current Pesos (million)	(4) GDP Price Index	(5) Forestry Depreciation	(6) GDP	(7) "Net Domestic Product"	(8) Forestry Depreciation as % of GDP
1970	−364.2	5.73	−2087	83.2	−2508	51014	48506	4.92
1971	−358.2	6.31	−2258	91.2	−2476	53672	51196	4.61
1972	−317.1	6.68	−2119	100.0	−2119	56464	54345	3.75
1973	−453.1	6.76	−3061	118.8	−2577	60202	57625	4.28
1974	−593.8	6.79	−4032	141.1	−2858	64187	61330	4.45
1975	−601.8	7.24	−4356	167.6	−2599	68437	65838	3.80
1976	−603.9	7.38	−4457	183.0	−2435	73922	71487	3.29
1977	−755.3	7.35	−5548	196.5	−2824	78467	75643	3.60
1978	−771.1	7.31	−5640	214.6	−2628	82784	80156	3.17
1979	−1128.3	7.32	−8263	247.3	−3341	87962	84621	3.80
1980	−1617.5	7.45	−12057	285.9	−4217	92568	88351	4.56
1981	−1387.9	7.83	−10873	317.3	−3427	96207	92780	3.56
1982	−1017.0	8.46	−8607	344.0	−2502	98999	96497	2.53
1983	−897.0	11.13	−9979	384.4	−2596	99921	97325	2.60
1984	−797.2	16.57	−13210	575.4	−2296	93927	91631	2.44
1985	−890.5	18.54	−16505	681.5	−2422	89904	87482	2.69
1986	−809.9	20.26	−16408	692.6	−2369	91287	88918	2.60
1987	−962.3	20.42	−19648	741.6	−2649	95948	93299	2.76

Note: Export exchange rate and GDP data are from the National Statistical Coordination Board, 1990.

This watershed estimate is based on the cost of replacing or preventing the nutrient loss associated with erosion, rather than the value of lost income. While the latter is the preferred approach for evaluating erosion costs, the erosion and crop acreage maps needed to construct such estimates are not available. However, to provide a crude assessment of the magnitudes involved, the productivity loss estimates for Indonesian upland crops were applied to Philippine crop data.

Rice, corn, and coconut are the three most important crops in the Philippines. Coconut trees protect the soil much better than do corn or upland rice (David, 1988). In 1987, P26 billion worth of rice or 8.5 million metric tons (mt) were harvested from 3.3 million hectares. Of this area, only 5 percent was in the uplands (David and Otsuka, 1990). Upland yields averaged .65 mt per hectare, compared to 2.62 in lowland areas. So upland rice production was about 107 thousand mt, worth P326 million (NSCB, 1990).

Corn was planted on 3.7 million hectares, with a total harvest of 4.3 million mt, worth P12.2 billion in 1987. No national estimate is available for the percentage of corn harvested in upland farms, but a conservative assumption is that 50 percent of corn production, worth about P6.1 billion in 1987, is from upland farms. Thus, the production of rice and corn from upland areas was worth about P6.4 billion. In Indonesia, the erosion cost in a single year, as a fraction of the value of rainfed agricultural output was about 4 percent.[15] Using this factor for rice and corn in Philippine upland agriculture, the loss due to soil erosion for 1987 was P257 million. Since this represents a continuing loss of productivity, the loss associated with soil depreciation for the year is P2.57 billion (P257 million capitalized at 10-percent interest). Deflated by the GDP price index in Table 2.9, this amounts to P346 million in 1972 prices.[16]

A similar calculation for 1970 was based on rice acreage of 156 thousand hectares, which produced a total harvest of 65 thousand mt, worth P26 million. The value of upland corn output was P263 million. From the total crop value of P289 million, the estimated productivity loss due to erosion was P11.6 million, with a capitalized value of P116 million. Using the GDP price index as deflator, this loss is equivalent to P139 million in 1972 prices. These estimates indicate rising erosion losses between 1970 and 1987.

Soil erosion in watersheds also affects downstream hydropower and irrigation systems. At present, the Philippines depends on hydropower from multipurpose dams for 37 percent of electricity generation, up from about 23 percent in 1981. Most national irrigation projects, which account for 42 percent of the total irrigated area, use dams and reservoir systems in key watersheds (NSCB, 1989). Sedimentation and water flow variability problems are increasing in many systems, but few potential new dam sites are left (David, 1988). The sedimentation of multipurpose reservoirs reduces storage capacity and service life and adversely affects irrigation and hydropower services. These losses were found to be small relative to on-site costs in two large multipurpose dam projects in Northern Luzon (W. Cruz et al. 1988).[17]

The only national estimates of off-site erosion impacts are those in the Philippine Forestry Masterplan (DENR, 1989). This "masterplan" found that off-site impacts affect mostly three sectors: irrigated agriculture, coastal fishing, and hydropower generation. The cost to irrigated agriculture amounts to 15.5 percent of total value of irrigated rice production, or P3.5 billion in 1988.[18] These losses were attributed to changes in water flows (12.4 percent), increased flooding (2.1 percent), and siltation (1 percent). Coastal fishing production declined by 5.9 percent, worth P935 million, due to sedimentation and water quality deterioration. For hydropower, only a general assumption of a 3-percent decline in power generation, equal to losses of P466 million per year, was possible.

The losses in these three off-site sectors add up to P4.9 billion for 1988 alone. However, because hard data to support many of the assumptions on which these estimates are based were lacking, the DENR study stressed the preliminary nature of the results. Consequently, only the on-site soil depreciation estimates for rice and corn were included in the consolidated depreciation table. *(See Table 2.6.)* However, it should be borne in mind that the excluded off-site costs may be as much as an order of magnitude greater.

Coastal and Fishery Resources

Mangrove forests, coral reefs, and inshore fisheries have been exploited ever more heavily in the Philippines. Mangroves have been cut for charcoal and fuelwood, and since the late 1970s they have been cleared to make way for brackish-water fishponds. Mangroves have declined to about a third of their extent at the turn of the century. Basing its estimate on SPOT survey data, the World Bank (1989b) reports that only about 149,000 hectares of widely scattered mangrove forests are left.

Coral reefs, which are critical in sustaining fish stocks, have also deteriorated significantly. A survey of more than 600 sites throughout the country found most reefs to be in only *fair* or *poor* condition, while coral reef conditions are *good* to *excellent* in other survey areas in the Indian Ocean and in the South Pacific. Most of the damage to Philippine coral reefs is caused by siltation from soil erosion (Gomez, 1980). Destructive fishing techniques, such as the use of dynamite, poisons, and *muro-ami*,[19] also degrade the reefs.

The loss of mangroves and coral reefs, together with over-fishing, have depleted coastal fishery stocks. *(See Table 2.10.)* Although the national fish catch increased from about 25,000 to about 400,000 metric tons by the mid-1980s, fishing effort per ton harvested almost tripled. Demersal fish biomass is estimated to have declined from about 930,000 tons between 1946 and 1949 to only 285,000 tons between 1980 and 1984 (Silvestre and Pauly, 1987).

Using bio-economic models, Silvestre and Pauly (1987) estimated that at the close of the 1960s, demersal fisheries yielded their maximum economic rent (MER). Using 1970 average municipal fishery prices, reported in the 1989 Statistical yearbook, their MER estimate is equivalent to 210 to 336 million pesos. This implies that if by 1970 fishing effort had been controlled at about the 1969 level to conserve the stock, the fishery could have continued to yield a yearly rent equal to P210 to P336 million. The mid-point of this estimate, P273 million, was used as the measure of rent for 1970. The asset value of this stream of rents is P2.73 billion.[20]

However, fishery rents declined from 1970 on, and in 1984 all rents were dissipated (Silvestre and Pauly, 1987). So, from a capitalized value of P2.73 billion in 1970 it can be assumed that rent declined linearly and disappeared altogether in 1984. The yearly loss from the decline of the fishery is the difference between the capitalized rent from one year to the next, or P195 million annually.[21] Adjusted to 1972 prices, this depreciation estimate of P234 million represents roughly 10 percent of current fishing output.[22]

Table 2-10. Annual Catch and Fleet Effort for the Philippines, 1946–1984

Year	Demersal Catch* (metric tons)	Standard Fleet Effort (trawler HP)	Catch per Unit of Effort (mt/trawler HP)
1946–49	58198	43127	1.35
1950–54	97337	103561	0.94
1955–59	138980	90566	1.53
1960–64	165809	201406	0.82
1965–69	249444	283497	0.88
1970–74	311394	606612	0.51
1975–79	373895	550952	0.68
1980–84	374241	810767	0.46

*These are average annual harvests for each period.

Source of basic data: Silvestre and Pauly (1987).

C. Investment and Resource Flows

The preceding sections document how resource assets declined while external liabilities grew in the last two decades. What happened to the resources generated by external borrowing and liquidating domestic natural resource assets? This section shows that these resources went mostly to inefficient industrial investment or were dissipated through capital flight. They were not invested in agriculture or other more productive uses.

The resources generated by external borrowing and liquidating domestic natural resource assets went mostly to inefficient industrial investment or were dissipated through capital flight.

Net Disinvestment from Agriculture and Natural Resource Sectors

From the late 1960s to the mid-1980s, there have been net resource transfers out of agriculture. The overvaluation of the peso was the principal transfer mechanism. Since many agricultural products are internationally traded, their export prices in pesos were severely reduced by peso overvaluation. Overvaluation, combined with industrial protection, raised the prices farmers paid for manufactured goods and lowered the prices they received for agricultural commodities. Other mechanisms included taxes, industrial subsidies, and price controls on agricultural products. Such output and input price interventions from 1967 to 1984 led to net transfers *out of* agriculture amounting to more than 10 percent of gross value added (GVA) in the sector. If the effect of the peso overvaluation is included, the net outflow amounted to more than 28 percent of agricultural GVA (Intal and Power, 1990).

During the same period, government gave substantial support to infrastructure and irrigation development in agriculture, but these inflows were not large enough to neutralize the disincentive to agriculture. Even if these government inflows were included in the assessment, total net outflows are still as large as 24 percent of agricultural GVA for the period 1976 to 1982 (Intal and Power, 1990).

Capital formation in agriculture increased during the period, mainly due to government irrigation investments, but remained below 10 percent of gross value added in the agricultural sector (David et al., 1984). *(See Table 2.11.)* Investment in agriculture has also been declining as a percentage of total gross domestic capital formation (GDCF), to less than 5 percent during the 1970s, though agriculture generated close to one third of GDP throughout this period. If estimates for forestry and fisheries investment are added to the figures for agriculture, and resource depreciation in all three sectors are subtracted, the picture appears even bleaker. *(See Table 2.12.)* Net investment in the primary sector was actually negative throughout the 1970s and early 1980s.

Industrial Investment

Disinvesting in the primary sector in order to inject capital into manufacturing was a poor recipe for sustained economic growth. Total factor productivity in the manufacturing sector, defined as the ratio of real outputs to factor inputs, declined by nearly one percent per year from 1956 to 1980 (Hooley, 1985). Increasing incremental capital-output ratios (ICOR) during the 1970s clearly show how inefficient investment in industry had become. *(See Table 2.13.)*

Capital Outflows

While the industrial investments had a poor productivity record, at least capital remained in the economy where it served some economic purpose. However, since the mid-1970s, capital outflow has been substantial and capital flight has been the major component of the outflow.

25

Table 2-11. Capital Formation in Agriculture, 1955–83

Year	Gross Domestic Investment in Agriculture (GDIA) (in million 1972 pesos)			GDIA/ Total Gross Domestic Capital Formation (%)
	Private	Irrigation	Agric. Total	
1955–59	269.06	51.90	302.92	6.73
1960–64	451.68	25.28	468.44	7.45
1965–69	505.30	29.64	534.94	5.43
1970	494.70	94.40	589.10	5.44
1971	466.20	135.60	601.80	5.36
1972	101.20	189.00	290.20	2.50
1973	37.50	266.50	229.00	1.83
1974	889.60	301.20	1190.80	7.61
1975	644.20	437.60	1081.80	5.70
1976	234.80	409.40	644.20	3.18
1977	919.80	433.50	1353.30	6.50
1978	679.50	577.60	1257.10	5.44
1979	1270.20	634.00	1904.20	7.23
1980	434.30	617.20	1051.50	3.95
1981	626.50	570.40	1196.90	4.40
1982	728.60	562.20	1290.80	4.89
1983	148.60	459.20	607.80	2.43

Source: Intal and Power (1990).

(*See Table 2.14.*) Capital flight was about as large as total gross domestic capital formation (GDCF) between 1981 and 1986.

* * *

In summary, government policy lowered the returns on investment in the primary sector, even though its contribution to exports, income, and employment was large. Overexploitation and inefficient use of natural resources in agriculture, forestry and fisheries reduced the capitalization of the sector. Private investment in agriculture, forestry and fisheries was too small to offset this capital consumption and did not increase significantly in the past two decades. Only government irrigation investment prevented major declines in the ratio of investment to agricultural value-added.

The government strategy in the Philippines was to direct investment toward industry in order to stimulate economic growth. However, the slow growth and high cost of manufacturing industries undermined the strategy. The government responded, not by altering its strategy, but by borrowing more heavily from abroad. As crisis approached, capital flight further reduced the Philippine economy's capacity to withstand the 1979 oil price shock and the world recession of the early 1980s.

Table 2-12. Net Disinvestment in Agriculture and Natural Resources
(in million 1972 Pesos)

Year	Gross Investment in Agriculture, Forestry, Fishery	Natural Resource Depreciation	Net Investment in Agriculture, Forestry, Fishery
1970	1,111	2,881	−1,770
1971	1,136	2,861	−1,725
1972	547	2,516	−1,969
1973	432	2,987	−2,555
1974	2,247	3,280	−1,033
1975	2,042	3,033	− 991
1976	1,215	2,881	−1,666
1977	2,553	3,282	− 729
1978	2,372	3,098	− 726
1979	3,592	3,824	− 232
1980	1,985	4,712	−2,727
1981	2,258	3,934	−1,676
1982	2,436	3,021	− 585
1983	1,147	3,127	−1,980

Notes: 1. Gross investment in Agriculture, Forestry, and Fishery is based on column 4 of Table 2.11, divided by .53, since agricultural investment is about 53% of primary sector investment.

2. Natural Resource Depreciation is from Table 2.6.

Table 2-13. Sectoral Incremental Capital-Output Ratios, 1970–82

Period	ICORs		
	Total	Agriculture	Industry & Services
1950–59	2.63	N.A.	N.A.
1960–69	4.11	N.A.	N.A.
1970–74	3.51	1.81	3.92
1975–82	5.47	2.37	6.37
1983–88	9.48	N.A.	N.A.

Notes: 1. ICOR is the ratio of fixed capital formation in the current year to the increase in GDP over the previous period. Agriculture includes fishery and forestry.

2. Sectoral investment data is not available up to the late 1960s. Thus, only total ICOR is presented. These period averages are the averages of yearly ICOR estimated by the World Bank (1976).

3. 1970–74 ICORS are based on sectoral investment estimated by World Bank (1976) and sectoral gross value added from *Philippine Statistical Yearbook*.

4. 1975–82 ICORS are based on (a) agricultural capital formation estimates of Intal and Power (1990), adjusted to include fishery and forestry, using Annual Survey of Establishments data on gross investment, and (b) *Philippine Statistical Yearbook* for sectoral gross value added.

5. 1983–88 Total ICOR does not include ICORs for 1984–85, which are negative (averaging −2.77). The peak ICOR is for 1983–84 (25.06), with 1986–88 averaging 4.28.
Source: National Statistical Coordination Board (1990).

Table 2-14. Capital Outflow (cumulative totals in million dollars for given years), 1962–1986

Year	Estimate of Capital Flight	Non-Flight Capital Outflow	Total Outflow	Capital Flight as Percent of Total Outflow
1962–69	1,560	15	1,575	99
1970–75	920	611	1,531	60
1976–80	3,798	114	3,912	97
1981–86	3,167	1,933	5,100	62

Source: Boyce and Zarsky (1988).

Part III. Intersectoral and Interregional Resource Reallocations

A. Overview

Development planning and macroeconomic policy in the Philippines have been crafted with little attention to the problems of industrial concentration and environmental degradation. The conventional view is that economic growth and poverty issues are the important policy concerns while the environment is the concern only of the rich. In fact, environmental damages exacerbated by misguided policy significantly reduce current as well as future productivity. Resource degradation also directly reduces consumer welfare, especially in poorer communities.

The spatial concentration of industrial activity and population in metropolitan centers generates pollution and increases its economic impact. In Metro Manila, because it is so overcrowded with people and factories, pollution grossly exceeds nature's assimilative capabilities and affects the health and welfare of millions of people.[23]

As early as the mid-1970s, a World Bank assessment of Philippine economic development identified the problem of growing industrial concentration in Metro Manila. However, neither the broad environmental implications of congestion nor the fundamental role of trade and import-substitution policies in promoting industrial concentration were recognized. The solutions proposed therefore emphasized project-oriented dispersal of infrastructure and power-generation investments. The World Bank's 1976 assessment was, in fact, overly optimistic about the prospects for decongesting Manila: "Government is already making noteworthy progress in shifting the geographic concentration of investments."[24]

Because the environment can assimilate low levels of pollution, early industrialization programs typically ignore externalities and save scarce capital by using unpriced environmental services. Industry produces excessive effluents, waste, and gases, which are then discharged into rivers, public landfills, and the air. At later stages of development, pollution affects production sectors and consumer welfare enough to create a demand for government regulation. If, however, the economy stagnates or the development process is arrested, pollution becomes more difficult to control. Environmental regulations or taxes are consistently rejected, not only by private industry (as expected) but even by government planners. Investment to improve environmental quality is postponed, leading eventually to lower levels of productivity and welfare in the future.

Partly for these reasons, current standards-oriented regulations in Manila are difficult to monitor and enforce.[25] In addition, macroeconomic policies promoted material-intensive technologies and industrial agglomeration. The import-substitution strategy and industrial protectionism have resulted in the growth of materials-intensive finishing industries prone to waste-generation. Government incentives, reliance on imported intermediate inputs, and proximity to consumer markets have encouraged industries to locate in Metro Manila. As a result, firms and households crowd the metropolis, creating excessive demands on environmental assimilative capacity and aggravating pollution.

B. Industrial Pollution and Spatial Concentration

The Effects of Industrial Promotion Policies

Both fiscal and trade policies have stimulated industrial waste and pollution generation. The Board of Investments provided tax exemptions and credits to eligible enterprises in the manufacturing sector. Aside from coconut milling and wood products, the industries that received the largest subsidies during the 1970s were all pollution prone and energy-intensive. These included pulp and paper, copper, steel, chemicals, and petroleum products.[26] *(See Table 3.1.)*

Trade and exchange rate policies have had even greater potential impact on Philippine firms' propensities to pollution because they change relative input costs, thereby broadly influencing resource allocation and technology choice. Specifically, the shift from primary to secondary production increased intermediate input use. In addition, the import-substitution program raised the prices of finished goods but kept intermediate inputs inexpensive. This shift in relative prices favored even more materials-intensive production methods.

The extent to which trade-related incentives favor a particular industry can be measured by its effective rate of protection (EPR)—the extent to which value added in the industry is increased or reduced directly by tariffs or indirectly by the tariffs on its inputs.[27] For example, during the mid-1970s, consumption goods had the highest average EPR, 77 percent, compared to an average rate of 44 percent for all manufactured goods. Intermediate inputs and capital goods had significantly lower protection rates—23 percent and 18 percent, respectively.[28]

Among major industry groups, manufacturing, whose average EPR was 44 percent of value added, had the highest protection rate, compared to 9 percent for agriculture and natural resources. Classified in terms of export orientation, industries that exported more than 10 percent of their production had the lowest average EPR of 4 percent, compared to an average EPR of 61 percent for non-exporting industries. While overall protection has declined, the EPRs for 1985 and even up to 1988 in Table 2.5 *(in Part II)* suggest that this foreign-trade related incentive structure, which encourages the use of intermediate goods, still persists.

These macroeconomic incentives have promoted the adoption of material-intensive activities and inefficient use of intermediate inputs. The trend in manufacturing factor productivity from 1956 to 1980 demonstrates the pervasive effect of this incentive structure. *(See Table 3.2.)* The ratio of output to intermediate inputs *declined* by 1.36 percent per year, which implies that, though manufacturing output was growing, the increase in intermediate inputs was even larger.

As industrial production became increasingly material-using, the industrial waste stream grew rapidly, because of greater discharge of residuals, more energy use, and more post-consumer waste.

As intermediate input use increased rapidly during the period under study here, these inputs were substituted for both labor and capital. From 1956 to 1970, manufacturing production

Table 3-1. Board of Investments Subsidies

Product	Tax Exemptions	Tax Deductions	Tax Credits
I. Agro-Based	**P34,847**	**P99,448**	**P1,084**
Fruit production	242	9,110	5
Livestock production	57	2,012	222
Marine products	1,635	899	
Cassava starch cornstarch	442	2,074	
Coconut oil*		34,140	
Processed coconut products and byproducts	200	687	
Processed food and beverage products	4,727	3,828	409
Ramie	7,321	2,231	
Fiber products	602	4,038	126
Wood and wood products*	2,726	25,194	257
Pulp and paper; pulp of straw and abaca*	16,883	14,984	28
Paper products			21
Handicrafts	12	251	8
Leather products			8
II. Mining and Mineral Products	**77,456**	**45,227**	**1,261**
Iron ore	1,881		106
Copper*	57,477	29,432	227
Nickel, silicate ore			72
Primary steel*	17,505		
Rock aggregate			371
Dinnerware		2,763	89
Ceramics, ceramic products		1,064	34
Glass products, laminated safety glass			
III. Metal-Based	**18,974**	**2,899**	**3,269**
Machinery, equipment and parts	1,123	122	15
Metal products	3,561	445	1,290
Electrical equipment, electrical products			
IV. Chemical-Based	**52,292**	**22,664**	**18,260**
Industrial chemicals, chemical and chemical products*	30,335	3,230	3,183
Petroleum products*			
Synthetic fibers	15,804	7,942	109
textiles, textile products	3,360	5,395	4,890
Synthetic bags		4	40
Plastic products	69	223	110
Medicinal and pharmaceutical products			573
Garments	2,724	5,870	8,765

*Largest Subsidies   Source: Bautista et al (1979).

Table 3-2. Total Factor Productivity Growth and Selected Partial Productivity Measures, 1956–1983 (All data in percent)

Production per Unit of:	1956–60	1961–65	1966–70	1971–75	1976–80	1981–83	1956–70	1971–80	1956–80
Labor	5.55	3.27	4.87	0.59	−4.04	−3.35	4.56	−1.93	2.05
Capital	0.78	2.95	2.89	1.37	2.72	**	2.21	2.04	2.15
Intermediate Goods	−0.51	−2.58	−0.26	−1.50	−1.86	**	−1.15	−1.68	−1.36
TFP	1.18	−0.71	1.22	−0.55	−1.90	−2.13	0.56	−1.23	−0.15

Source: Hooley (1985).

grew at 10.2 percent per year, while intermediate inputs grew even faster at 11 percent per year. From 1971 to 1980, production growth was only 6.6 percent per year, but input growth was 8.9 percent per year (Hooley, 1985). As industrial production became increasingly material-using, the industrial waste stream grew rapidly, because of greater discharge of residuals, more energy use, and more post-consumer waste.

Geographic Concentration and Pollution Trends

Not only did the industrial waste stream grow rapidly over these decades, it also became increasingly concentrated in Metro Manila. Various forces concentrated population and industry in Manila. Among macroeconomic factors, the most important were industrial promotion policies that channelled manufacturing growth toward import-substitution by protecting the domestic market. Since the domestic market is concentrated in Manila, consumer goods industries located there. The heavy use of imported intermediate inputs also encouraged proximity to Manila's main seaports (Pante and Medalla, 1990).

The government's investment program also promoted regional concentration. In a mutually

supporting fashion, infrastructure development in Manila led to industrial development and, consequently, to even more concentration of social services and facilities. For example, a disproportionate share of transportation and communication infrastructure and utilities are found in Manila. Close to half of all public investment goes to energy, transportation, and communication, the bulk of which is destined for Manila and adjoining regions. Even in the current public investment plan, this area will also get a third of the regional investment funds (NEDA, 1989).

This locational bias was so strong that even agro-processing firms converged on the metropolitan area. Corn, most of which is grown in the southern island of Mindanao, is the principal raw material for the feedmilling industry. Because transportation facilities are limited, it is more than twice as expensive for feedmillers in the main island of Luzon to buy corn from Mindanao than to have it shipped to Manila from Thailand (Cabanilla, 1990). Thus, even though its clientele is rural, this industry is concentrated around Manila.

Historical data on the regional distribution of manufacturing employment show increasing industrial concentration in Manila *(see Table 3.3.)* Before 1940, less than a third of manufacturing employment was in the area. After the

Table 3-3. Distribution of Manufacturing Employment by Region (in percent), 1903–1987

Year	Central/Manila	Traditional/Agricultural	Frontier
1903	30	67	3
1939	31	56	13
1948	47	41	12
1961	68	20	12
1967	64	19	17
1975	65	21	15
1987	69*	n.a.	n.a.

Note: Estimates for 1903 to 1975 are based on Hermosa (1983), using census data. For 1987, the estimate comes from DENR (1989) and refers to industrial establishments as a proxy for industrial employment.

industrial promotion program was initiated in the 1950s, manufacturing employment in Manila jumped to more than two-thirds of the total (Hermosa, 1983). In the most recent survey of manufacturing establishments, 69 percent of all manufacturing firms were located in Manila or in the adjoining regions (DENR, 1989b).

Increasing Pollution and Environmental Degradation

Only in the late 1970s was it recognized that a thorough reform of the industrial promotion system was needed "to modify the extreme regional concentration that currently exists."[29] In 1982, when two thirds of industry had already located in Manila, the World Bank identified the trade and exchange rate regime and the allocation of fiscal incentives as the primary factor leading to the congregation of import-substituting firms in Manila.[30] By then, however, it was much too late to be starting a program to alleviate the pattern of congestion and pollution in Metro Manila.

Among a sample of 11 countries in Asia, the Philippines already has the dubious distinction of having an extremely large primacy ratio,

even though it consists of an archipelago.[31] The index for the Philippines was 3.71 vs. 1.48 for Indonesia, 1.17 for Korea, and 1.49 for Taiwan. Only Thailand, in fact, had a higher index in the sample.[32] This excessive concentration exacerbates the impacts of industrial and household pollution, many of which are already too costly to remedy.

About 7 million people and 69 percent of the country's 15,000 industrial firms currently crowd 636 square kilometers of land in Metro Manila (DENR, 1989b). According to government estimates, Manila's households and factories generate about 3,600 tons of solid waste per day (DENR, 1989). Other assessments place the amount at 7,000 tons, with only 65 percent collected by the city (World Bank, 1989b). Although environmental monitoring information is limited, available data suggest a continuing decline in environmental quality.

The sewerage system, originally designed before World War II, serves only a fraction of the current population. According to DENR, about 12 percent of the city's population is connected to the system. However, according to Metropolitan Water and Sewerage System data, 48,754 sewer connections link only 106,384 households—or 1.4 percent of the area's total—to its network (Delos Angeles and Lasmarias, 1990). Most households directly dump waste water into Manila's river systems, contributing about 70 percent of the biodegradable organic pollutants (UNEP, 1986).

Wastewater is discharged with little or no treatment from the 10,350 industrial firms in the area. These include many pollution-prone enterprises, such as chemical plants, paper mills, tanneries, distilleries, and food processors. Worse, toxic effluents are discharged by most factories without any apparent treatment (DENR 1989b).

As a result, all of Metro Manila's five river systems are biologically dead, and the situation is deteriorating. Data from water-quality monitoring sites in four of the area's five river systems show a declining trend in dissolved oxygen (DO) levels. In 1978, DO was 3 to 4 milligrams per liter (mg/l), compared with 1.5 to 4 in 1982 and 0 to 2.5 mg/l in 1987. A dissolved oxygen content of 5 mg/l is generally required to support aquatic life. In Manila Bay, water quality is no longer suitable for shellfish production or even for recreation. Bacteriological data shows increasing levels of total coliform, from 263 to 72,954 MPN/100 ml in 1982 to 8,306 to 5,503,821 MPN/100 ml in 1989. By contrast, the standard for recreational class waters is 1000 MPN/100 ml (Palanca and Balagot-Gan, 1990).

Data on ambient air quality are even more limited. However, an increasing trend in air pollution is evident from the mid-1970s. While sulfur dioxide is still not considered a critical problem, annually averaging well below 0.05 parts per million, commuters are nonetheless regularly exposed to excessive concentrations of 1,000 mg/cubic meter of respirable suspended particulates (RSP) (DENR, 1989b).

For total suspended particulates (TSP), 11 monitoring stations throughout Metro Manila have tracked growing pollution. In 1977, TSP was less than 100 ug (micrograms) per cubic meter. In 1986, all monitoring stations had TSP readings that exceeded the 180 ug per cubic meter standard. By 1989, TSP ranged from 345 to 2,580 ug per cubic meter for the two most polluted areas (Palanca and Balagot-Gan, 1990).

Because of congestion, environmental degradation is most acute in the Metro Manila area. Trade and industrial policies promoted pollution and energy-intensive production processes and contributed to the concentration of both factories and households in the area. With both industrial and population congestion, the negative effects of pollution on human welfare are magnified.

C. Macroeconomic Constraints on Energy Conservation

Although macroeconomic policies, including the overvaluation of the local currency, favored the use of imported petroleum, the massive increase in oil prices, together with sectoral energy diversification and conservation programs, succeeded in reducing energy intensity in the Philippines. Petroleum imports increased until during the 1970s they accounted for close to one third of all imports. However, energy consumption (in tons of oil equivalent) per unit of GDP (in million U.S. dollars) decreased from 433 in 1970 to 356 in 1980 (World Bank 1987). At the same time, energy sector programs promoted the development of non-petroleum and indigenous sources of energy. Domestic energy production increased from only 6 percent in 1975 to 27 percent in 1987 based on substantial growth in hydropower and geothermal sources (World Bank, 1987).

Input cost adjustments and new taxes increased fuel prices substantially after the first and second oil price shocks. *(See Table 3.4.)* These price adjustments in the Philippines were generally larger than those in other Asian countries.

Similar price adjustments were delayed for the power sector. Although electricity rates did rise to cover the operating cost of power

Table 3-4. Price Changes of Petroleum Products, 1973–1981
(in percent)

	1973–75		1979–81	
	Philippines	Average	Philippines	Average
Kerosene	194	40	87	59
Gasoline	260	70	121	61
Bunker Oil	250	47	118	133

Note: Average refers to 10-country mean percentage change. The countries are Burma, India, Pakistan, Sri Lanka, Philippines, Thailand, Indonesia, Malaysia, Korea, Singapore.

Source: W.T. James (1983).

generation, these were still about 30 percent lower than the long-run cost associated with the need for additional generating capacity.[33] Thus, the National Power Corporation has continually received the largest subsidy among state corporations.

Although the record of sectoral energy policies was mixed, at least the general policy direction was toward energy conservation. However, macroeconomic policy worked at cross-purposes. The major incentive to energy use was the real appreciation of the peso relative to the dollar and its role in petroleum imports. Before 1972, the peso was consistently overvalued. As Table 2.3 *(in Part II)* showed, it actually appreciated in 1973–74 and in 1979–82[34] especially important periods because they coincide with the adjustment period after major increases in petroleum prices. Thus, instead of depreciating the peso to transfer the impact of higher oil prices, government policy kept the peso relatively overvalued—14 percent to 24 percent greater than the free-trade equilibrium value for 1962–86 (Intal and Power, 1990).

Instead of accepting the needed peso depreciation, government opted for more external borrowing. During the 1979 oil price increase, for example, government adopted policies to expand exports, substitute for imports, and reduce

somewhat its economic growth targets. But these moves only countered one-fourth of the oil price shock, with the difference between the gains from adjustment and the higher import bill paid for by net capital inflows (Power, 1983). Net imports were not sufficiently reduced.

The import-substitution program provided additional incentives for petroleum use. Tariff protection allowed the prices of manufactured goods to rise at the rate of increase in the nominal tariff. Because of preferential tariff treatment, the price of intermediate inputs for petroleum products increased more slowly than those of other manufactured goods. Relative to the rest of manufacturing, some of the most energy-intensive industries—iron and steel, non-ferrous metals, and cement—also gained from tariff-related incentives for imported inputs (Hooley, 1985).

Although, on balance, significant progress was made in controlling the absolute increase in energy use and in reducing dependence on imported energy, more could have been accomplished, and probably with greater efficiency, if the real increase in petroleum cost had been allowed to change the structure of imports and input use. Instead, the burden of energy conservation was placed fully on sectoral pricing and domestic energy development programs.

Part IV. Poverty, Population Pressure and Environmental Degradation

A. Population Pressure on Marginal Resources

In the Philippines, most land suitable for intensive agriculture is low-lying. About 14.1 million hectares of lowlands, with slopes less than 18 percent, are officially classified as "alienable and disposable."[35] About 8.6 million hectares of "marginal" lands have slopes between 18 to 30 percent. These can be cultivated but require appropriate land-conservation practices, such as fallowing, mulching, or terracing, for sustained crop use. Permanent crops represent the best use of many such areas. About 6.5 million hectares have slopes above 30 percent, and are suited only for forestry. Officially, both marginal and forested areas are classified as "forest" lands. Unlike the alienable and disposable lowlands, these cannot be transferred to private owners, but must remain under the jurisdiction of the Department of Environment and Natural Resources (DENR). (The term "uplands" refers to both marginal and forest lands.)

Although crops can be grown on marginal lands or even on forest lands, doing so generates substantial off-site environmental costs. Soil erosion can damage irrigation and power facilities downstream, reduce water quality, and aggravate seasonal flooding. Erosion also reduces upland soil fertility, so that agriculture can be maintained, if at all, only by increasing input use. Large areas previously forested have already been converted into farms, and agriculture continues to expand in the uplands, accelerating soil erosion (World Bank 1989b; DENR, 1989a). In the 1960s, cultivated area in the uplands amounted to only 10 percent of lowland cropped area, but by the 1980s it had increased to about 40 percent. The upland cultivated area has increased on average by at least 7 percent per year for the past three decades. *(See Figure 4.1.)*

Rapid Population Growth

Population growth and the increase in the rural labor force underlie the expansion of upland subsistence farming. Population more than doubled in the past three decades, and rapid population growth continues. Population density has reached 208 persons per square kilometer, and arable land declined to only about half a hectare per person in 1980. *(See Table 4.1.)*

From 1945 to 1965, agricultural output increased primarily through acreage expansion. Rice output, for example, grew by 2.2 percent annually from 1955 to 1965; acreage grew by 1.4 percent per year; but yield increased by only 0.8 percent per year. After 1965, when lowlands that could be easily converted into agriculture were eventually exhausted, higher yields were achieved by introducing modern rice varieties, irrigation, and fertilizer. From 1965 to 1985, during the so-called "green revolution," rice output expanded by 3.7 percent per year, with 3.5 percent coming from yield

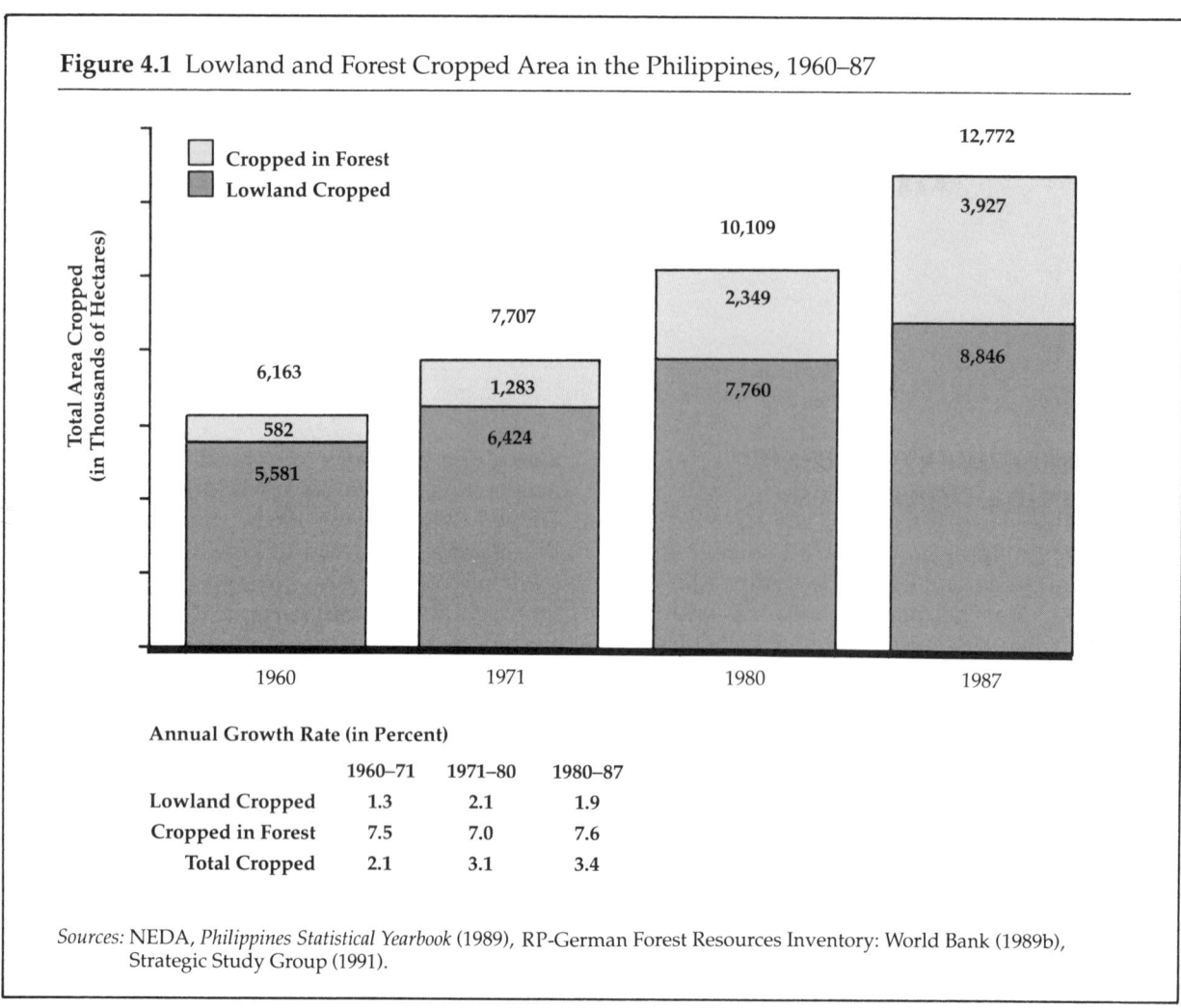

Figure 4.1 Lowland and Forest Cropped Area in the Philippines, 1960–87

Cropped in Forest
Lowland Cropped

Total Area Cropped
(in Thousands of Hectares)

12,772
3,927
8,846

10,109
2,349
7,760

7,707
1,283
6,424

6,163
582
5,581

1960   1971   1980   1987

Annual Growth Rate (in Percent)

	1960–71	1971–80	1980–87
Lowland Cropped	1.3	2.1	1.9
Cropped in Forest	7.5	7.0	7.6
Total Cropped	2.1	3.1	3.4

Sources: NEDA, *Philippines Statistical Yearbook* (1989), RP-German Forest Resources Inventory: World Bank (1989b), Strategic Study Group (1991).

growth and only 0.2 percent attributable to acreage increase (David and Otsuka, 1990).

However, the green revolution only temporarily averted the problems of rapid population growth and an increasingly severe constraint of land availability. The green revolution technologies depended on irrigation development,[36] but by the 1970s the best dam sites were occupied and finding new sites suitable for irrigation became more difficult. Costs per hectare for new irrigation developments increased. Up to the 1960s, rice yields averaged 1.25 tons per hectare. With the spread of high-yielding varieties (HYVs) and with irrigation

development, yields grew rapidly. From 1975 to 1980, yields grew by more than 5 percent per year.[37] Growth decelerated in the 1980s since many farms had already adopted HYVs, and new irrigation development became increasingly costly.

High-yielding varieties (HYVs) were adopted first in the most favorable farm areas, and in the 1970s yields were highest for irrigated farms. By 1980, HYV adoption was almost complete in irrigated and favorably situated rainfed farms. Yields were still much higher than in unfavorable areas, but yield growth had stopped.[38] The continuing growth in average

Table 4-1. Population Density and Arable Land, 1960–90

	Population (thousands)	Growth Rate	Density (persons/sq. km.)	Arable Land per Person Employed in Agriculture (ha/person)
1960	27088.00	3.06	90.30	0.94
1970	36684.00	3.01	122.30	0.72
1980	48098.00	2.71	160.30	0.53
1990	62400.00	2.48	208.00	n.a.

Sources: National Census and Statistics Office for 1960, 1970, & 1980. *WRR 1990–91* for 1990 population, growth, and density.

yield after the 1970s occurred in unfavorable areas where HYV adoption was slower. As the green revolution ran out of steam, therefore, the earlier pattern of achieving agricultural growth by expanding acreage reappeared, but now with more extensive cultivation of increasingly marginal lands.

Limited Employment Generation

In agriculture, the period of rapid labor absorption coincided with the years of rapid yield growth in the late 1970s, but even during these years underemployment in the whole economy increased. *(See Table 4.2.)* After 1980, when growth in lowland agriculture slowed, employment generation lost momentum too. Thus, except for the 1960s, the labor force grew faster than employment.

Employment grew too slowly to take pressure off marginal resources, mainly because industrial employment decelerated from 3.37 percent per year during the 1960s to 2.94 percent per year in the 1970s and 1.9 percent per year between 1980 and 1985. *(See Table 4.3.)* Typically, industry siphons off the rural labor force as economies develop. However, the share of industry in total employment fell in the 1960s before settling at about 15 percent of total employment in the 1970s. From 1960 to 1970, for every 10-percent rise in industrial output, industrial employment rose by only 4.1

percent. The comparable figure decreased to 3.8 percent during the 1970s. Although employment increased during the crisis years of the early 1980s, underemployment exceeded 35 percent of total employment in 1984. As a result, real wages fell by about 25 percent between 1981 and 1987 *(see Table 4.3)* and the fraction of the population below the poverty line increased. *(See Table 4.4).*

Agriculture provided a residual source of employment. Its sectoral employment elasticity increased from 0.31 in the 1960s to 0.66 in the 1970s. *(See Table 4.5.)* During the crisis, it absorbed even more employment relative to sectoral production. This process, however, increased underemployment in lowland agriculture and further pressured the underemployed to migrate onto marginal uplands and coastal areas.

B. Poverty and Migration to the Uplands

While rapid population growth and lagging labor absorption constitute the basic sources of pressure on marginal resources, poverty and the accessibility of forest lands and coastal resources promote continuing migration to these areas. Influences on migration are categorized either as ''push'' or ''pull'' factors. Underemployment and low wages ''push'' households out of overcrowded, low-income

Table 4-2. Labor Force and Employment Trends, 1960–88

	Labor Force	Total	Employment Agriculture	Industry	Services
			(Thousand Workers)		
1960	10,076	8,828	5,379	1,331	2,060
1970	12,378	11,989	6,200	1,911	3,844
1980	17,308	16,434	8,453	2,554	5,421
1985	21,318	19,801	9,698	2,812	7,292
1988	23,451	21,497	9,920	3,348	8,227
			(Growth in %/year)		
1960–70	2.08	3.11	1.43	3.37	6.44
1970–80	3.41	3.20	3.15	2.94	3.50
1980–85	4.26	3.15	2.79	1.94	6.11
1985–88	3.23	2.78	0.76	5.99	4.10

Sources: 1. 1960–70 Labor Force data are from World Bank (1976). 1980–88 data are from 1989 *Philippine Statistical Yearbook.*

2. Total and sectoral employment data are from *Philippine Statistical Yearbook,* various issues.

areas. The possibility of acquiring access to land in newly opened areas ''pulls'' settlers who don't expect productivity and incomes to decline so quickly in the uplands.

The Role of Poverty

The ''push'' factors are reflected in the trends and regional variations in poverty incidence. Studies of the percentages of households below absolute poverty lines based on minimum food requirements or basic needs show that there has been little progress in alleviating poverty in the Philippines. In the early 1970s, 49 percent of the population fell below the poverty threshold. *(See Table 4.4.)* By the mid-1980s the figure reached 58 percent.[39] By this measure, development efforts had failed.

Not only did the overall poverty rate increase throughout the 1970s and early 1980s, a consistently greater proportion of rural than urban

households fell below the poverty threshold. Although agricultural intensification in the Philippines increased returns to irrigated lands, rural wages stagnated or declined. In the lowlands, the green revolution rice technology increased labor demand. Early maturing, high-yielding varieties allowed more crops per year to be grown on the same land, and higher yields required more harvesting and threshing work (Hayami et al., 1976; Barlow et al. 1983). However, because farmworkers were mobile and population growth was rapid, wages remained low. If labor demand in one region increased as the result of new irrigation development, workers migrated there to find work. Reservoirs of underemployment in less productive areas kept wages low, even though average output per worker increased.

The green revolution primarily increased returns to land, the scarce factor. Owners of irrigated lands benefitted especially because the

Table 4-3. Wage and Unemployment Trends, 1975–1988

	Unemployment (in %)				Real Wages (in 1979 Pesos)	
	Total	Urban	Rural	Total Under-Employment	Metro Manila Non-Agricultural	National Non-Plantation Agricultural
1975	4.2	7.8	2.6	–	12.9	9.3
1976	5.2	8.5	3.5	–	13.9	9.5
1977	4.5	7.2	2.2	–	15.4	10.8
1978	4.1	6.0	3.2	–	15.9	11.4
1979	4.0	–	–	–	17.2	12.1
1980	5.0	8.2	3.7	34.5	19.4	12.3
1981	5.3	8.3	4.0	36.3	19.8	12.3
1982	6.0	9.8	4.2	34.2	18.1	11.4
1983	5.4	9.3	3.7	35.9	17.5	11.1
1984	6.2	10.7	3.5	35.7	16.6	10.5
1985	7.1	11.8	4.4	33.7	16.2	10.1
1986	6.7	11.5	3.9	36.0	15.4	10.1
1987	9.4	13.8	6.8	30.5	14.7	10.0
1988	8.3	12.3	5.9	29.4	16.8	12.5

Sources: 1. For unemployment data: National Statistical Coordination Board (1990).

2. For wages data: Reyes and Sanchez (1990) using National Wage Commission data, Department of Labor and Employment.

new technology required water control. Yields improved much more in irrigated and favorable rainfed areas than in unfavorable sites, creating rents that were captured by landowners rather than by the government. In the Philippines, water charges accounted for only 10 percent of returns to irrigation (Repetto, 1986).

At the same time, lack of industrial employment opportunities depressed urban real wages. In the highly protected organized sector, wages increased substantially during the 1970s, but underemployment in the informal sector remained high and earnings differentials large.[40] Stagnant wages and pervasive underemployment meant that a large fraction of the total population, urban and rural, remained poor.

The government neither enforced its own regulations against converting forest areas to agriculture, nor enforced the tenurial rights of traditional communities indigenous to the uplands.

Income and poverty differentials prompted substantial internal migration flows. People migrated out of impoverished regions to regions offering better prospects. Table 4.6 suggests poverty is a migration push factor while higher income, measured as regional domestic

Table 4-4. Poverty Thresholds and Incidence, 1971–85

Year	Poverty Line (Pesos/yr./family [in 1978 pesos])			Poverty Incidence Per Capita (% below poverty line)		
	Rural	**Urban**	**Total**	**Rural**	**Urban**	**Total**
1971	363.0	485.0	400.0	56.0	37.0	49.0
1985	4132.0	6042.0	4764.0	62.0	50.0	58.0

Source: NEDA Medium Term Plan (1989).

product per capita, attracts in-migration or discourages out-migration.[41]

The Pull of "Open Access" Resources

The uplands attract migrants because settlers can obtain squatters' rights on agricultural holdings. The government neither enforced its own regulations against converting forest areas to agriculture, nor enforced the tenurial rights of traditional communities indigenous to the uplands. In this sense, which is as much political as institutional, the uplands can be considered open access resources.[42] Coastal fisheries can also be considered open access resources since traditional communal limits on resource use have been overridden and ignored.

Exploiting open access resources can be quite profitable in the beginning. Newly cleared uplands still retain fertile topsoil. Since there are no land owners to demand rent or a share of output, all returns from cultivation go to the settler. However, with each subsequent harvest, soil degradation reduces yields, and each year more migrants compete for available lands. Eventually, labor use expands on the available land until the average cost of labor is just covered by average productivity—all resource rents are dissipated.[43] In short, poverty drives agricultural workers from crowded farmlands, but poverty also awaits them in fragile uplands.

Not surprisingly, the highest percentages of poor workers are landless or dependent on

In short, poverty drives agricultural workers from crowded farmlands, but poverty also awaits them in fragile uplands.

open access resources. The incidence of poverty among farm part-owners and tenants during the period of study was 50 to 56 percent and among fishermen and related workers it was 54 percent. In contrast, poverty incidence for all other occupations was 6 to 44 percent (Quisumbing and Cruz, 1986). Data for later years used slightly different occupational categories, but in general the same occupations—farmers, fishermen, and landless workers—had the highest incidence of poverty in 1982 and 1983. Workers in farming and fishing experience such high rates of poverty in part because they lack secure access to productive resources.

C. The Impact of Macroeconomic Policy on Unemployment and Poverty

Macroeconomic policies intensified the problems of absorbing the rapidly growing work force productively, exacerbating pressure on marginal resources. Policies constrained labor absorption in general and depressed agricultural

Table 4-5. Responsiveness of Employment to Changes in Sectoral Output, 1960–88

	Agriculture	Industry	Services
Gross Value Added (million 1972 Pesos)			
1960	9,338	6,354	11,464
1970	14,821	15,592	20,341
1980	23,662	33,472	35,434
1985	26,252	29,000	34,652
1988	27,771	33,205	40,558
Employment (000 persons)			
1960	5,379	1,331	2,060
1970	6,200	1,911	3,844
1980	8,453	2,554	5,421
1985	9,698	2,812	7,292
1988	9,920	3,348	8,227
Employment Elasticity			
1960–70	0.31	0.41	1.09
1970–80	0.66	0.38	0.62
1980–85	1.32	−0.68	−13.50
1985–88	0.40	1.29	0.77

Note: Employment elasticity is the percentage change in employment divided by percentage change in gross value added.

Source: Philippine Statistical Yearbook, various issues.

incomes in particular. Trade taxes and an over-valued peso penalized export industries, especially labor-intensive agricultural and manufacturing activities (Bautista et al, 1979; Intal and Power, 1990). Measures of effective protection, for example, indicate that there was low or even negative protection of agricultural and export-oriented activities[44] (David, 1983; Intal et al., 1987; David et al., 1986; Intal and Power, 1990). Calculated with reference to a projected equilibrium trade balance, the peso was over-valued by about 20 percent during the mid-1970s. Since agriculture is a relatively labor-intensive exporting sector, this overvaluation penalized the sector and more than offset the effects of government's irrigation and agricultural price support programs, thus reducing rural employment and incomes (Intal and Power, 1989).

Government's industrial promotion program also discouraged investment in agriculture. Inducements to manufacturing investments during the 1970s included accelerated depreciation, the carry-over of losses, tax exemptions on imported equipment, tax credits on domestic equipment, tax deductions for plant expansion, and generous tax exemptions for "pioneer" enterprises. These incentives encouraged investment in industry, where it generated relatively less employment than in other sectors. (David, 1983). The industrial promotion program also "cheapened" capital because tax credits were allowed for capital use (Manasan,

Table 4-6. Poverty Incidence and Migration by Region, 1980

	Per Capita GDP (pesos at 1972 prices)*	Poverty Incidence (percent)	Net Migrants 1975–1980 (thousands)
1. Ilocos	989.00	40.30	−52.8
2. Cagayan Valley	981.00	43.10	−2.5
3. Central Luzon	1466.00	27.40	10.6
4. Southern Tagalog	1820.00	31.30	67.9
5. Bicol	783.00	42.70	−63.6
6. Western Visayas	1422.00	50.50	−73.8
7. Central Visayas	1509.00	48.10	−64.9
8. Eastern Visayas	718.00	33.00	−72.9
9. Western Mindanao	1130.00	40.10	−8.8
10. Northern Mindanao	1368.00	38.60	35.4
11. Southern Mindanao	1605.00	33.30	27.2
12. Central Mindanao	1395.00	28.40	17.9
National Capital Region	3893.00	11.20	180.3
All Regions	1655.00	14.30	0

* Real Gross Domestic Product (GDP) in 1972 prices.

Sources: National Economic and Development Authority, National Income Accounts and *Philippine Statistical Yearbook*, 1980; migration figures adjusted by Nguiangain (1986).

1990). As a result, labor-capital ratios declined in almost all industries between 1960 and 1980 (Pante and Medalla, 1990).

Macroeconomic factors also contributed to income inequality and poverty. Import quotas and investment incentives allowed influential individuals to gain monopolistic control in industry and make high profits. During an address to the Philippine Economic Society, President Marcos' former economic planning minister concluded:

Some parties, through their closeness to the powers that be...were able to get their foreign exchange and import allocations rather cheaply. The assembly plants that they built were thought to be the beginnings of a sound industrialization. But in effect, they were largely fed by imported raw materials. They also borrowed capital very cheaply...through the development finance institutions set up by government. Hence, these industries received the highest form of protection...to monopolize a limited market.[45]

Taxation did little to relieve poverty, partly because the Philippine tax system became more regressive between the late 1970s and early 1980s[46] (Habito, 1990). About 70 percent of tax revenues are generated from indirect taxes, which fall disproportionately on the poor (Habito, 1988).

The proportion of indirect to direct taxes in the agricultural sector was greater than for the rest of the economy, largely because agricultural land taxes are limited. The maximum tax rate is 3 percent of land value, but even at that, assessments are underestimates of market values and tax collection is generally less than 50-percent effective. This land tax, among all those levied on agriculture, could have made agricultural taxation more progressive. However, strong landowner opposition prevented any reforms (Habito and Manasan, 1990). Thus, regressive taxes fell particularly heavily on the rural poor.[47]

Rural credit rationing, made unavoidable by government-controlled interest rates, directed institutional finance mostly to larger farmers. Interest rate controls were rationalized to protect poorer borrowers from richer lenders, but fewer than one third of the subsidized agricultural loans reached small farmers (Neri and Llanto, 1985). Most small farmers and rural producers had to depend on the informal credit market, where interest rates ranged from 32 to 230 percent per year.[48] The anti-usury law set an interest rate limit of 12 percent on secured loans and 14 percent on unsecured loans, resulting in negative real interest for savings and poor mobilization of domestic savings by the banking system (ILO, 1974).[49] Since lending was constrained, banks and financial institutions channelled funds to well-established borrowers with substantial collateral. Because risks are generally higher in agriculture, bankers' credit-rationing strategies restricted the funds it provided to the sector, confining their lending mainly to larger farmers.

Government attempted to correct the problem by creating a subsidized credit system, but this was directed mostly to the industrial sector. Although total outstanding agricultural loans from 1981 to 1988 ranged from P26 to P30 billion, this total represented only 8 to 9 percent of all loans by the financial system (Lamberte et al., 1989). The main recipients of government loans were construction and capital-intensive industries (Remolona et al., 1986).

National Policies Regarding Land Tenure

National policies on land reform and the use of public lands had major effects on labor markets, factor shares, and income distribution. No national data on land ownership are available, but the maldistribution of agricultural lands can be inferred from available data on farm size distribution. Figure 4.2 shows Lorenz curves for the distribution of agricultural land by farm size. Such a curve is easily interpreted. If it coincides with the diagonal, land distribution is perfectly equal: 10 percent of land is owned by 10 percent of farms, 30 percent of land is owned by 30 percent of farms, and so on. The farther a curve is from the diagonal, the more unequal is land distribution. For example, in 1960, farms that were below 3 hectares in size comprised 62 percent of all farms, but accounted for only about 25 percent of total agricultural land. In general, the figure shows, land distribution is quite unequal and there was no significant improvement between 1960 and 1980.

The shared tenancy system and landlessness continue to be the main causes of rural poverty and inequality in the Philippines. The failure of land-reform programs has been a persistent cause of poverty. The Marcos government professed the ambitious goal of transferring ownership of all tenanted rice and corn farms larger than 7 hectares to the tenants. However, for the 10-year period of Marcos' land reform, 1971 to 1981, the number of farms under tenancy arrangements increased from 289,418 to 581,456. Some transfers of rice farms occurred, but in corn-growing areas, where land is easier to convert to other crops, landlords switched out of corn to other crops and avoided land redistribution (Quisumbing and Cruz, 1986).

The number of landless agricultural workers indicates more directly that access to farmland was restricted. As the amount of arable land available per person employed in agriculture declined from 0.72 hectares in 1970 to 0.53 hectares in 1980, the number of landless workers increased from 40 percent of all agricultural workers in 1975 to 56 percent in 1980[50] (Philippines Department of Agriculture, 1988).

Increasing migration inflows intensifed the need for clear tenurial policies in the uplands

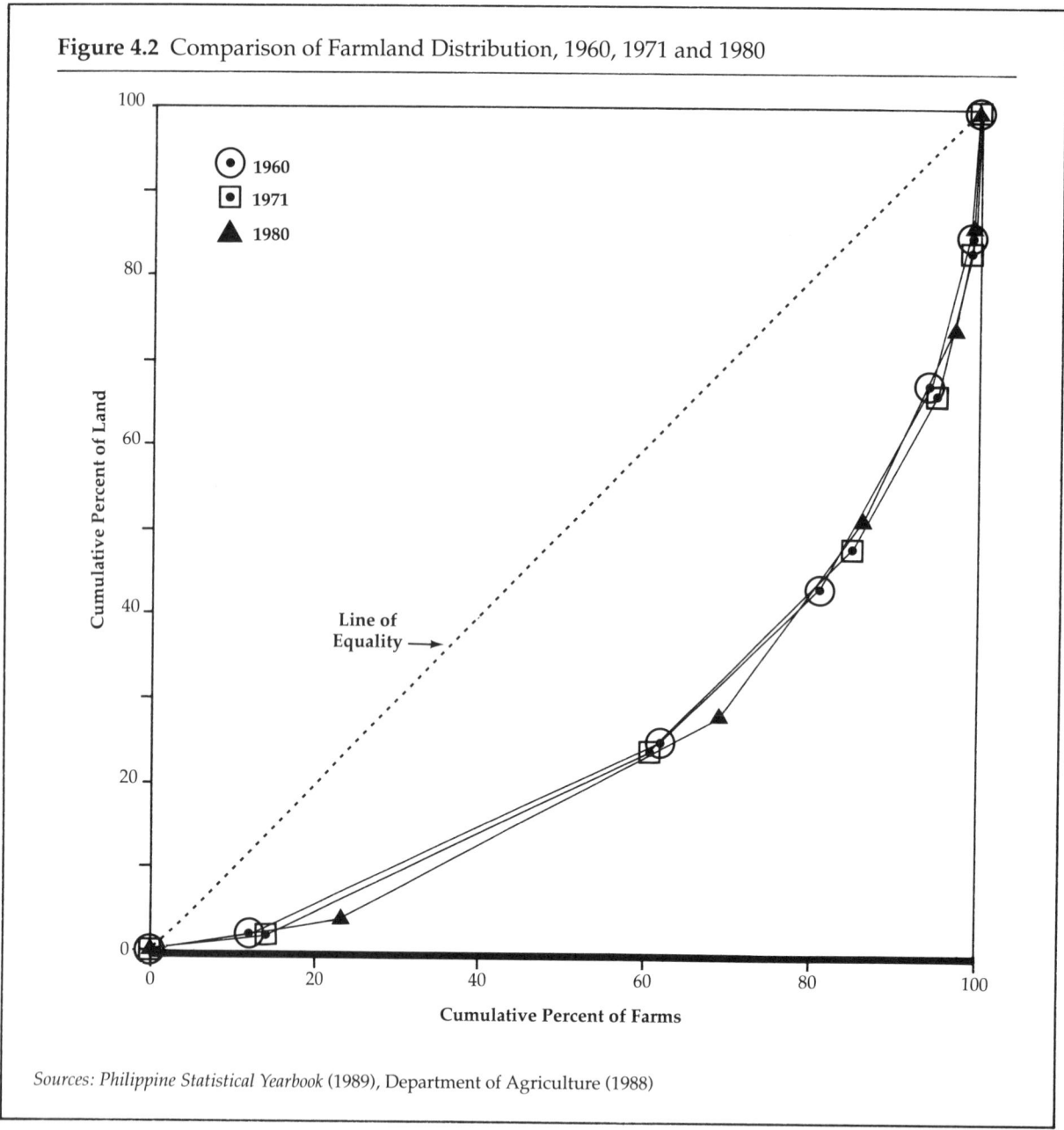

Figure 4.2 Comparison of Farmland Distribution, 1960, 1971 and 1980

- ⊙ 1960
- ⊡ 1971
- ▲ 1980

Cumulative Percent of Land

Line of Equality →

Cumulative Percent of Farms

Sources: Philippine Statistical Yearbook (1989), Department of Agriculture (1988)

and coastal fishing areas. Yet, at present, these resources still belong to the state, and the rights of the overwhelming majority of upland farmers and coastal fishermen to the use of natural resources are insecure. Upland communities and fishing villages suffer because most exploitation rights were allocated to a small number of concessionaires.

In the uplands, more than 15.9 million hectares, 53 percent of the country's land area, are classified as forest land, but the forested proportion of such lands has severely declined in the past two decades. In 1987 the forested area totalled only about 4.3 million hectares, or 27 percent of what is classified as forest land. Within forest lands, 5.4 million hectares are covered by Timber License Agreements (TLAs), which were granted to about 130 logging concessionaires (DENR 1988).[51] The average TLA covers 40,000 hectares and runs for 50 years, including renewals. As of 1987, an additional 441,640 hectares of forest lands were allocated to 1,115 grazing permit or lease-holders (DENR, 1988).[52]

Thus, a minuscule proportion of the population controls more than one third of all public lands. Remaining areas have mostly become effectively open access resources, available for exploitation by the poor and the unemployed.

Together, 1,245 forest concessionaires and grazing permit holders control 5.8 million hectares of public lands. Thus, a minuscule proportion of the population controls more than one third of all public lands. Remaining areas have mostly become effectively open access resources, available for exploitation by the poor and the unemployed.[53] Alongside the thousand or so officially permitted exploiters of forestlands are more than 17 million upland dwellers, most of whom practice subsistence farming (C.J. Cruz et al., 1988). Because they lack secure claims on the sites they occupy, they have little incentive to adopt land-conserving farming practices.

The artisanal fishery involves a much smaller population, but growth rates of fishing households and employment have been very large. Between 1970 and 1980, households dependent on fishing increased from 275,865 to 581,670, an annual growth rate of 7.8 percent. The total number of fishermen increased from 375,658 to 1,054,645, for an annual growth rate in excess of 10 percent. Case studies of key coastal fishing areas, San Miguel Bay in the Bicol region

and Lingayen Gulf in Pangasinan and La Union provinces also suggest very large labor inflows during the last two decades. The catch has been declining in the last 5 years even though fishing effort has increased (Pauly, 1989). Consequently, returns to labor have dropped. Between 1971 and 1985, the proportion of fishing households below the poverty line increased from 53.6 percent to 71.5 percent, the highest incidence of poverty among all occupations (World Bank, 1988a).

D. The Effect of the Economic Crisis on Migration

The worst effects of the debt crisis and the contractionary policies adopted under the stabilization program carried out from 1983 to 1985 were their adverse effects on unemployment, poverty and income distribution. Unemployment averaged 6.57 percent during the 1960s but declined somewhat to 5.44 percent from 1970–74.[54] However, overt unemployment rose from 4 percent at the start of the crisis in 1979 to 6.2 in 1984 and 7.1 percent in 1985. *(See Table 4.3.)* Open urban unemployment reached 11.8 percent in 1985. Perhaps worse, underemployment, the proportion of those employed who worked less than 40 hours per week, affected more than one third of the total work force during the crisis—a better indication of the shortage of jobs.

Real wages in both agricultural and non-agricultural activities declined every year from 1980 until economic recovery started to take hold in 1987, falling by about 25 percent between 1981 and 1987. *(See Table 4.3.)* Rising unemployment and falling real wages raised the percentage of population living in poverty since the poor had nothing to offer but their labor.

Increasing peso overvaluation (Sicat, 1986) added to the detrimental effect by discouraging exports, which are labor-intensive to produce. The real effective exchange rate adjusts the nominal exchange rate for changes in tariffs and relative rates of foreign and domestic inflation. After 1979, the real effective exchange rate kept appreciating until the onset of the crisis in 1983, when it depreciated significantly. However, in 1984 and 1985 it again appreciated.[55] Thus, instead of alleviating poverty in the years leading to the economic crisis and in the two years immediately after, the exchange rate policy tended to further constrain employment generation and labor earnings.

The exacerbation of poverty during this period intensified population pressure on uplands and coastal fisheries. Population pressure was already evident in the 1970s. Before 1970, most migrants went from stagnating rural areas to other rural areas where agriculture was expanding rapidly. During the 1970s, migration shifted to Manila, which received more than half of all inter-regional migrants. However, during this period rural-to-rural migration also occurred from lowlands to upland sites (C.J. Cruz et al., 1988). The upland migration rate grew from 3.4 to 9.4 percent between 1970–75 and 1975–80. Substantial numbers of people migrated from the lowlands of the Central Philippines to the uplands of the southern island of Mindanao. Migrants also moved from the lowlands of Central Luzon to the mountain provinces in the north. (See Figure 4.3.) Migrants to the uplands converted most logged-over land into farms (C.J. Cruz et al., 1988).

This relocation process intensified during the crisis period. Net upland migration grew to 14.5 percent of total upland population during the period 1980 to 1985. This massive inflow of more than 2.5 million new migrants, most of whom depend on farming for subsistence, inevitably accelerated deforestation and soil erosion in the uplands. (See Table 4.7.)

Population pressure on coastal fisheries also intensified during the early 1980s. No direct information exists on changes in employment in fishing during the crisis period, but total artisanal fish harvests increased significantly and catch per unit of effort declined (Pauly, 1989). In contrast, commercial fishing remained generally stagnant during this period. This trend suggests that, because of increasing migration of poor households to coastal fishing areas and entry into artisanal fishing as a supplemental activity, the fisheries were increasingly over-exploited. Since artisanal fishing has always been a low-productivity occupation of households at the lowest income levels, this influx into artisanal fishing also suggests that the number of poor households increased.[56]

Development patterns that generated too few jobs and failed to provide acceptable incomes led to growing exploitation of fragile natural resources. Migration to the uplands was already in progress during the 1970s, though urban areas attracted more labor flows. The economic contraction occasioned by the debt crisis and the stabilization program created so much unemployment that migration patterns changed drastically. The large migration flows to Manila declined, and most migrants could turn only to open access forests, watersheds, and artisanal fisheries. Thus, the major environmental effect of the economic crisis was overexploitation of these vulnerable resources.

Figure 4.3 1980–85 Migration Flows

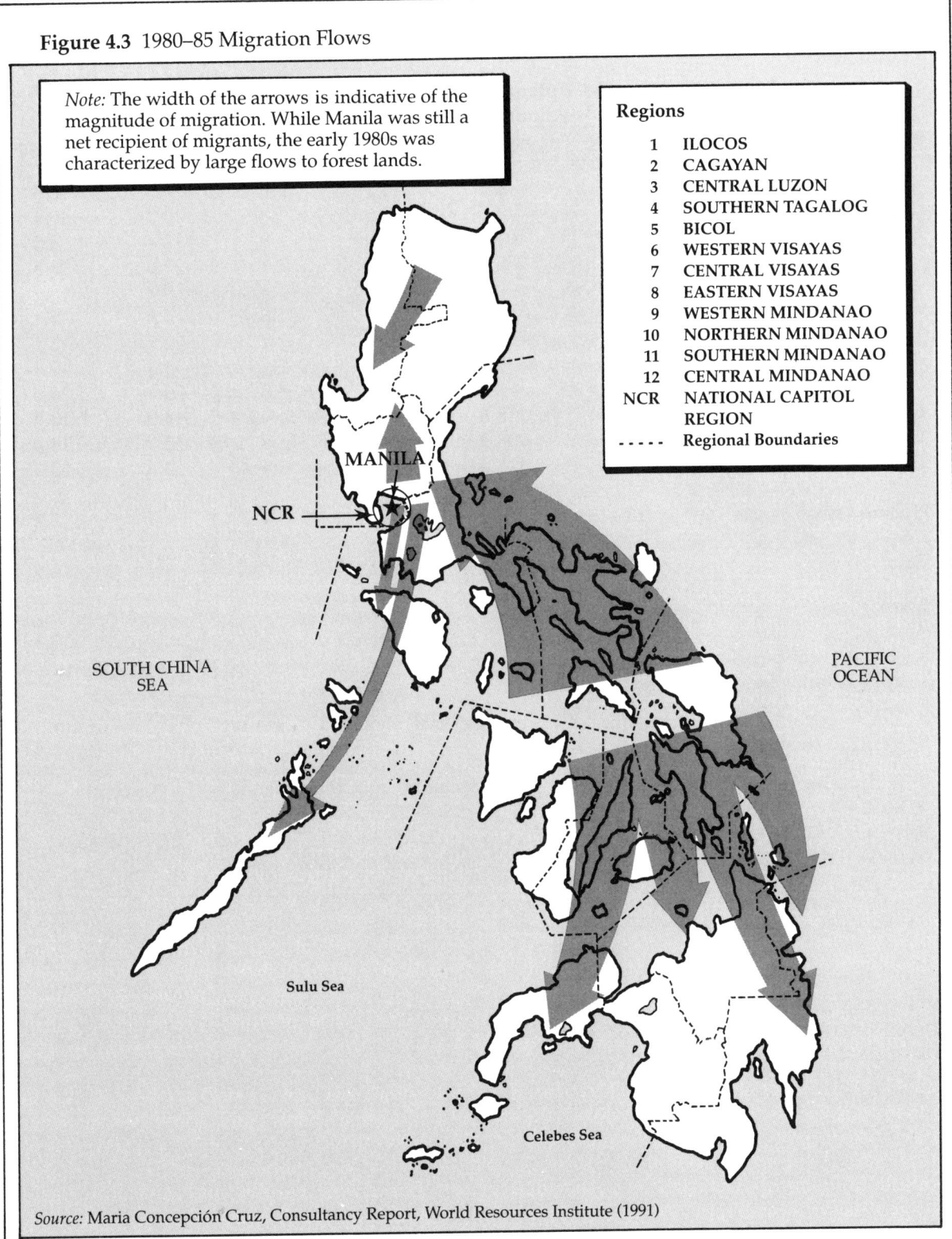

Note: The width of the arrows is indicative of the magnitude of migration. While Manila was still a net recipient of migrants, the early 1980s was characterized by large flows to forest lands.

Regions

1	ILOCOS
2	CAGAYAN
3	CENTRAL LUZON
4	SOUTHERN TAGALOG
5	BICOL
6	WESTERN VISAYAS
7	CENTRAL VISAYAS
8	EASTERN VISAYAS
9	WESTERN MINDANAO
10	NORTHERN MINDANAO
11	SOUTHERN MINDANAO
12	CENTRAL MINDANAO
NCR	NATIONAL CAPITOL REGION
- - - - -	Regional Boundaries

MANILA

NCR

SOUTH CHINA SEA

PACIFIC OCEAN

Sulu Sea

Celebes Sea

Source: Maria Concepción Cruz, Consultancy Report, World Resources Institute (1991)

Table 4-7. Patterns of Upland Migration in the Philippines 1970–85

Region	Net Upland Migrants[a] (thousands)			Net Upland Migration Rate[b] (percent)		
	1970–75	1975–80	1980–85	1970–75	1975–80	1980–85
1. Ilocos	30.3	−4.1	276.5	2.3	−0.3[c]	16.8
2. Cagayan	17.5	−3.5	152.9	1.8	−0.3	10.4
3. Central Luzon	14.8	104.5	93.9	2.0	12.4	8.5
4. Southern Tagalog	23.7	285.8	306.5	2.1	22.0	18.5
5. Bicol	−15.8	−2.3	−1.3	−1.1	0.2	−0.1
6. Western Visayas	−22.1	−66.5	−1.7	−1.6	−4.5	−0.1
7. Central Visayas	36.7	−50.1	−22.4	−2.2	−2.7	−1.1
8. Eastern Visayas	−19.0	−60.0	−32.6	−2.2	−6.4	−2.9
9. Western Visayas	93.1	−2.2	182.5	20.2	−0.4	24.0
10. North—Mindanao	51.3	175.6	174.8	4.9	14.0	10.8
11. South—Mindanao	94.7	238.3	405.5	6.3	12.9	18.3
12. Central Mindanao	43.4	173.3	225.6	6.4	23.6	23.7
Upland Urban Areas	152.1	575.0	785.3	3.1	6.3	7.2
Total	427.3	1,363.8	2,545.5	3.4	9.4	14.5

Notes:

a. Net migrant population, including lowland-to-upland and upland-to-upland movements, less upland-to-lowland transfers.

b. Net migration rate is the number of in- and out-migrants as a percentage of the total population in the uplands.

c. A negative figure indicates net outflow of population from the uplands.

Sources: National Census and Statistics Office, Population Census, 1970, 1975, 1980; Barangay Census, 1985; adjusted for uplands by Cruz, Zosa-Feranil and Goce (1986).

Part V. The Environmental Impact of Stabilization and Adjustment Programs

A. The Economic Crisis and Adjustment Programs

Stabilization policies aim to correct short-run balance of payments and budgetary deficits; structural adjustment policies are intended to promote sustained economic growth (Yagci et al., 1985). Yet, stabilization and structural adjustment programs may involve similar policies. Both programs usually include: (1) policies to reduce aggregate demand—e.g., cutting public spending, increasing taxes, contracting the money supply; (2) policies to restructure the economy—e.g., trade and exchange rate reform, changes in the structure of public spending, tax reform, and measures to improve factor markets and factor mobility. However, the goals of stabilization policies will clearly be shorter term.

In the short term, the deflationary effects of stabilization policies can worsen unemployment, and spending cuts might fall heavily on the poor (Addison & Demery, 1988; Cornia et al., 1987). Of course, if such consequences of stabilization policies are compared with the effects of runaway inflation or economic collapse, they may seem the lesser of two evils. However, a more relevant comparison is with stabilization and structural adjustment programs designed to cushion the hardships inflicted on the poor (Blejer and Guerrero, 1990). Efforts are now under way to comprehend these "social dimensions" of adjustment policies.[57] However, there have been few assessments of the environmental effects of stabilization and adjustment lending.[58]

In the Philippines, the first structural adjustment program was motivated by the recognition, as early as the mid-1970s, that the economy's performance was lagging behind those of comparable Asian countries, even as external debt and trade deficits were increasing. Structural adjustment efforts were directed at such underlying weaknesses of the economy as inefficient investments, poor industrial performance, and dependence on a limited number of commodities as exports. Stabilization policies addressed recurring balance-of-payments problems culminating in the debt crisis of the early 1980s, and their implementation overlapped with that of the structural adjustment program.

Conditions Leading to the Debt Crisis of the Early 1980s

The buildup of external debt in the Philippines was discussed in Part II. An increasing share of external debt went to the public sector, from less than 40 percent in 1971 to more than 57 percent by 1983 (Remolona et al., 1986). Some of it clearly ended up in private overseas bank accounts (Boyce and Zarsky, 1988), but a substantial fraction of this borrowing was channelled to large low-yielding, long-term government projects. Funds were also lent through government banks to inefficient public corporations (De Dios, 1984). About 58 percent of the assets of the Philippine National Bank and 87 percent of the Development Bank of the Philippines became ''non-performing,'' primarily because of these loans. By 1984, the total government contribution to these public corporations exceeded 10 billion—a sum greater than the budget deficit (Montes, 1987).

After the second oil price shock in 1979, short-term foreign borrowing to finance oil imports rose from 16 percent of all foreign borrowing in 1971 to more than 22 percent in 1983 (Remolona et al., 1986). These loans softened the effect of the rise in oil prices on the economy and reduced the need for immediate domestic adjustments. Foreign borrowing also enabled the government to keep the peso overvalued, further reducing the economy's capacity to generate exports.

The Philippine economy was clearly in no condition to absorb further external shocks when world interest rates increased (as developed countries adopted tight monetary policy to control inflation) and international commodity prices fell. Interest rates climbed to double digits while Philippine export prices fell by 30 percent from 1980 to 1982. Borrowing to cover the growing trade deficits became unsustainable. The process collapsed when new loans dried up. In October 1983 the Philippines, having nearly exhausted its foreign exchange reserves, declared a moratorium on debt payments.

The Stabilization Programs

From 1979 on, the Philippines had recourse to several stabilization loans. The 1979 stand-by agreement involved a credit line of SDR 105 million, with two conditions: the government would exercise fiscal and monetary restraint to contain inflation and take steps to manage the petroleum price increase. In 1980, an SDR 410 million stand-by agreement included four performance targets: 1) a 30-percent cap on net credit increases to the public sector, 2) a limit on new external borrowing, 3) a limit on the

net domestic assets of the banking sector, and 4) a decrease in the banking system's net international reserves. The 1983 agreement, involving SDR 504 million, focused primarily on reducing the balance-of-payments deficit to $800 million on condition that government expenditures and transfers to government corporations would be reduced, taxes increased, and the expansion in total credit limited.

These agreements were intended to control the current account deficit indirectly by reducing the budget deficit. But the government failed to meet the agreed conditions and was not able to forge another stand-by arrangement with the IMF until crisis struck late in 1983. Then, the government was forced to control the budget deficit.

Although the peso was devalued at about this time, the Aquino assassination closed most foreign credit lines, and the government had to declare a moratorium on debt-servicing payments. The Marcos government nevertheless viewed the crisis only as the result of the loss of international credit, and it still considered itself powerful enough to regain its credit standing without making any real structural change in the economy. Its objective was to obtain a new IMF stand-by arrangement that would enable it to re-schedule debt payments with its commercial creditors. For this reason, it was prepared to comply with IMF requirements.[59]

In 1984, the Marcos government initiated many stabilization policies without waiting for an IMF formal agreement. The government reduced the monetary base, devalued the exchange rate, removed foreign exchange controls, increased interest rates, broadened the tax base, relaxed price controls, and created a peso-deposit system of debt servicing to support monetary targets. The peso-deposit system allowed public corporations to make debt-service payment through peso deposits to the Central Bank, which assumed the dollar liability. This system restricted the money supply since the deposits, raised from levies or increases in regulated prices, were not re-channelled back into the economy by the Central Bank. Such measures significantly reduced the government's deficits, with great contractionary effects (Krugman and Taylor, 1978).

A formal agreement was finally arranged with the IMF in 1984. (Table 5.1 documents the economic changes associated with the program.) In the third quarter of 1984, inflation reached an annual rate of 63.6 percent.

The 91-day treasury bill rate almost quadrupled within a two-year period and peaked at 42.2 percent in the last quarter of 1984. The rich were able to reduce their losses from inflation by purchasing these bills. For the rest, incomes collapsed. Real wages fell between 1983 and 1985[60] by 15 percent for agricultural workers and by as much as 21 percent for skilled workers. The resulting contraction in spending lowered output and employment. By 1985, the recession had reduced inflation to below 1983 levels.

Although aimed mainly at reducing demand, the 1984 program also attempted to pursue some structural adjustment goals. The government dismantled its foreign exchange allocation system, and devalued the peso from P8 to $1 to P11 in 1983 and P18 in 1984. However, the nominal devaluations were offset by rapid inflation. In 1985, once the IMF arrangement was finalized, the real exchange rate actually appreciated.

Tax reform, which the IMF considered a priority, was not undertaken within the program's short implementation period. Instead, regressive indirect taxes were used to raise government revenue. Import and export taxes were imposed but lifted as soon as program deadlines for trade liberalization neared. An attempt to increase taxes on income and wealth by updating real estate assessments from 1978 to 1984 met with such strong criticism that it was dropped (Habito and Manasan, 1990). Thus, in 1984 foreign trade and sales taxes still comprised 67 percent of government revenue

Table 5-1. Adjustment Targets vs. Actual Performance

		1983	1984	1985	1986
Current Account	projected		1.5	1.1	0.6
Deficit	actual	2.8	1.3	0	−0.9
($ billions)					
Gross Domestic	projected		22.0	22.5	23.0
Investment	actual	27.1	19.2	16.2	14.0
(% of GNP)					
Money Supply (M3)	projected		10	13	12
(% increase)	actual	19	7	10	6
Reserve money	projected		15	11	10
(% increase)	actual	49	12	8	22
Real GNP growth	projected		−6	0	n.a.
	actual	1.1	−6.8	−3.8	0.1
CPI Increase	projected		40–45	10–15	8–10
(end of period)	actual	26.1	50.8	5.7	−0.3

Source: Montes (1987) and NSCB (1990).

while income and wealth taxes made up only 26 percent.

On balance, stabilization policies were dominated by demand-reducing policies. The IMF's primary goal was to decrease the budget deficit. The government's, in contrast, was to protect favored interests. Both goals were met without substantial structural reform: the government raised new revenues from regressive taxes while condoning bad loans to political allies and continuing to fund inefficient public sector companies.

Structural Adjustment Loans

The World Bank's first structural adjustment loan to the Philippines (SAL I, 1980–83) was intended to liberalize the tariff structure, promote exports by improving the incentive system, simplify import procedures, and restructure selected industries.[61] The range of tariff rates was to be narrowed to 10 to 50 percent from 0 to 100 percent: up to 20 percent for raw materials, 20 to 30 percent for intermediate and capital goods, and 40 to 50 percent for consumer goods. In addition, import licensing for about 1,000 "non-essential" and "unclassified" consumer commodities would be removed, comprising about 75 percent of the items in the tariff code. To promote exports, a flexible exchange rate was to be adopted, and Board of Investments export incentives were to be simplified. In addition, deposit requirements for imported inputs of export industries were to be reduced or waived, and additional export-processing zones established throughout the country. Finally, excessive protection for 14 key industries were to be removed.

The second structural adjustment loan (SAL II, 1983–85) was implemented in 1983 to follow-up on SAL I. Its objectives were reforms in industrial promotion policy, an extension of trade policy reform, and changes in energy policy. The major reforms included redesigning investment incentives, continuing tariff reform, and adopting uniform indirect taxes on similar imported and local goods. An energy component was also included in SAL II because of the broad range of energy prices on the economy. The program's goals were to promote conservation and energy efficiency and to reduce the government's role in the energy sector.

Implementation of Structural Adjustment

The first structural adjustment loan program was designed to raise manufacturing growth from 6.5 to 8 percent per year and employment growth from 3 to 6 percent per year by 1985. Although most loan conditions were met, these goals were not attained, presumably because of world recession and the debt crisis. Indeed, the debt crisis hit so hard that many adjustment policies were sidetracked. For example, although tariffs were reduced, surcharges were imposed on imports: 3 percent in December 1982, 5 percent in April 1983, and 8 percent in March 1984.

In January 1981, peak tariffs were reduced to a maximum of 70 percent for 177 tariff items and rates were reformed for 14 industries (affecting 668 tariff items). Also, 264 out of 1,304 imports affected by licensing restrictions were liberalized.[62] Later in the year the government implemented tariff-rate reforms for three more industries involving 480 tariff items.

In January 1982, peak tariffs were cut again, this time to 50 percent, and quotas for 610 more imports were relaxed. The tariff reform and import quota abolition programs were essentially completed by 1985. With lower tariffs and no real devaluation of the peso, total imports increased by close to 5 percent from 1981 to 1982 and exports declined by 7 percent. The balance-of-payments situation rapidly deteriorated. The current account deficit grew from 5.4 percent to 8.1 percent of GDP (Intal and Pante, 1989).

Reforms of industrial promotion programs led to better short-term results. Thanks to these programs, economic assessment of projects became more rigorous and sectoral programming more focused. For example, only five months after the policy reform, 70 percent of new applications for industrial incentives involved export-oriented enterprises. The adjustment program also reduced disincentives for labor use, except for exporting firms. The substitution effect, measured as the reduction in labor use relative to a "no-incentives" base, declined from 44.5 percent to 16.0 percent for new non-exporting firms. However, for new exporting firms, the substitution effect increased slightly, from 21.1 percent to 23.7 percent (Manasan, 1989).

Conventional wisdom holds that the debt crisis, by intensifying the need for foreign exchange, has increased resource exploitation for export. This generalization is overly simplified.

Energy sector reforms also showed results. Before the crisis, oil made up 12 percent of imports, compared to 25 percent after the first oil price shock. As use shot up, the government responded by raising petroleum product prices and taxes to induce energy conservation and the substitution of local energy sources for imported oil. These domestic price increases were much larger than the average price increase in other Asian countries (except for bunker oil), and greater after the first oil shock than after the second.[63]

The second structural adjustment loan promoted energy conservation and oil import savings by setting up a broad energy investment plan involving a larger role for the private sector. Under the terms of this loan, electricity rates were increased to fully reflect long-run marginal cost, and cross-subsidies between gasoline and diesel fuel and between residential and industrial electricity use were removed. Higher electricity rates improved the financial situation of power companies. Oil imports decreased from 73 percent of all energy supply in 1981 to 65 percent in 1983 (Yagci et al., 1985).

B. Environmental Impact of the Debt Crisis and Adjustment Programs

The Impact of the Crisis on Resource Exploitation for Export

Conventional wisdom holds that the debt crisis, by intensifying the need for foreign exchange, has increased resource exploitation for export. This generalization is overly simplified. The debt crisis did indeed force countries to seek additional foreign exchange earnings. However, it was accompanied by sharp economic contractions in both industrial and developing countries, which reduced world demand for primary commodities. Internal consumption, international commodity prices, and export demand all declined in the early 1980s. As developing countries were attempting to increase primary commodity exports, local and world demand was falling. The net effects on production, which is what affects the environment, would be hard to predict.

Table 5.2 presents a decomposition of the changes in domestic production for eight key primary commodities in the Philippines between 1980 and 1985. The effects of changes in domestic consumption, export demand, and prices are distinguished. In general, the data do not support the proposition that resource exploitation intensified because of the economic crisis. On the contrary, in the Philippines domestic production of most primary commodities fell substantially, by much more than the decline in net exports. The large fall in domestic absorption accounts for the difference.

Logs and lumber production declined most. In part, this drop was due to government

Table 5-2. Changes in Resource-Based Production, 1980–85 (in million U.S. Dollars).

| | Change in: | | | |
	(1) Domestic Production	(2) Domestic Absorption	(3) Net Export Volume	Note: Item 3 excludes price effect below
Logs and Lumber	−596.3	−504.4	−91.9	−41.2
Refined Oil	−471.7	−667.8	−196.1	4.7
Sugar	−201.1	214.7	−415.8	−39.5
Copper Concentrates	−119.7	258.0	−377.7	−77.1
Fish Products	−17.4	−27.6	10.2	−13.8
Crude Oil	—	−477.2	477.2	104.5
Bananas	48.5	65.1	−16.6	15.6
Coconuts	54.8	−17.5	72.3	−293.2
Total	−1,302.9	−1,156.7	−146.2	−340.0

Note: ''Domestic absorption'' refers to all domestic use of commodities (for consumption or investment). ''Net export'' is exports less imports. The price effect is the component of net export value that is due solely to changes in the price of net exports.

Source: Adapted from Reisen and Van Trotsenburg (1988), Table II.31.

attempts to raise revenues through an export tax on logs. However, charges for cutting rights had been minimal, and the timber boom of the late 1960s and the early 1970s had already depleted timber resources. Thus, both supply constraints and declining demand limited production.[64] The same is true of the output of fisheries, which were already over-harvested when the crisis began: declines in domestic and foreign sales contributed to a production fall-off. Meanwhile, changes in energy policy helped reduce net imports as domestic energy use declined, so the production of petroleum products fell too. Domestic production of copper also decreased, entirely because export demand fell, since domestic absorption actually increased. Among the traditional agricultural exports, sugar production fell because external demand did, despite rising domestic consumption. Coconut production decreased as the result of a general decline in demand. Banana production, however, rose as domestic and foreign demand increased.[65]

These estimates indicate that, instead of being exploited more heavily to generate exports, the resource sectors actually contracted. The debt crisis was accompanied by a deep and wide-spread world recession, collapsing world commodity prices, and restrictive stabilization policies. For most resource sectors, particularly forestry and fishing, in which many years of over-exploitation had already limited potential yields, production dropped quite markedly.

Misplaced concern over the effect of the economic crisis obscured its truly disturbing consequences: the increased exploitation of fragile natural resources. As shown in Part IV, the environmental impact of the crisis worked through massive unemployment and income decline. Real wages dropped by more than 20 percent between 1983 and 1985, forcing drastic adjustments in the labor market. In search of subsistence, many workers migrated to the uplands and coastal areas, where they increasingly over-exploited damage-prone resources.

Misplaced concern over the effect of the economic crisis obscured its truly disturbing consequences: the increased exploitation of fragile natural resources.

The Environmental Effects of Adjustment Programs

A general equilibrium analysis is required to assess the environmental effects of structural adjustment programs because macroeconomic policies engender many indirect and cross-sectoral effects. Since none of the structural adjustment reforms dealt directly with resource management, their effects on resource use worked indirectly through changes in prices, outputs, and incomes. Therefore, for this analysis, a computable general equilibrium (CGE) model was adapted from macroeconomic data and models currently in use by the Philippine government and by the Philippine Institute for Development Studies (Habito, 1990). The model includes four basic sectors—industries, households, government, and an external sector. It identifies 14 producing industries. *(See Table 5.3.)* Although the environmental consequences of production activities are not modelled explicitly, particular sectors known to have significant environmental effects are distinguished. Corn and rootcrops are grown mostly in hilly areas, where they generate significant soil erosion. Forestry, as currently practiced, generally leads to deforestation. Over-fishing now occurs in most of the country's important fisheries. Mining, dominated by copper, depletes mineral reserves and, at the same time, pollutes downstream farmlands and coastal fisheries. Petroleum use and power generation give rise to pollution.[66]

Table 5-3. Production Sectors in the Computable General Equilibrium Model

Sectors:	Notes:
1. Rice	
2. Corn	
3. Coconut	Includes copra
4. Rootcrops	Mostly cassava
5. Coffee and Cacao	
6. Sugar, Livestock, Other Crops	Livestock refers mostly to hogs, cattle in farms
7. Fisheries	Includes inland, commercial artisanal fisheries
8. Forestry	Logging and related activities
9. Wood Products	Includes lumber, plywood, and furniture
10. Metal Mining	Mostly copper and gold
11. Non-metal Mining	Mostly copper and gold
12. Other Manufacturing	Includes all milling and refining
13. Energy	Mostly power and petroleum products
14. Services	Includes government services

Note: These sectors are identified in the Philippines input-output table (NEDA, 1983) from which information on their input use was derived.

Part IV established the relationship between unemployment and pressure on such marginal resources as forestlands and mangroves. Subsistence exploitation of these resources—shifting cultivation and fuelwood gathering, for example—are not included in the national accounts or input-output tables that form the empirical base of CGE models. Nonetheless, the implications of macroeconomic policies on these resources can still be assessed indirectly. For example, if policies exacerbate unemployment and poverty, labor-migration pressures on marginal resources increase. The model can evaluate such resource pressures by examining the effects of policy changes on income distribution since the model's household sector is subdivided into three income groups, each with its own consumption, saving, and employment patterns.

Factors of production in the model include land, labor, and capital. (Few other neoclassical CGE models include a land input.) Land contributes to production in each agricultural and forestry sector, but it was not feasible to distinguish varying qualities of land used for different crops. The model allows for substitutions among land, labor, and capital used in production, but not among intermediate inputs. The pattern of intermediate input use in 1983 forms the basis for fixed input-output coefficients. For the use of the land, labor, and capital, the producing sectors pay out income to the various household classes. The high-income classes obtain most of the capital and rental payments and the poor households receive mostly wages.

Government and an external sector make up the other major components of the model. The government generates revenues from direct and indirect taxes, state corporations, and transfers from abroad. In the model, the government then spends revenues on the output of the production sectors, according to fixed expenditure proportions. The external sector purchases exported goods at prices set at historical levels. Imports are purchased by both production sectors and households. (Appendix 5.2 describes the model in more detail.)

To simulate the general pattern of economic stagnation during the early 1980s, initial production, employment and other relevant economic quantities were based on 1983 data. A benchmark run was then carried out, recreating the conditions prevailing in 1983. To simulate the environmental effects of the various structural adjustment policies, the model was re-run with different policy variables (singly or in combination). Then, the resulting values of income, employment, and sectoral outputs were compared with the base case. The changes represent adjustments in the economy that would normally take place within a three- to five-year period. This medium- to long-term perspective reflects the time necessary for changes in investment and factor flows to work through the economy. The simulations concentrate on the most important areas of reform: trade, industry, agriculture, and energy.

1. Trade Liberalization and Devaluation

A recent theoretical analysis predicts that trade liberalization will exacerbate resource degradation by expanding sectors in which the environmental costs of production activities are not internalized (Lopez, 1991). Empirical simulations carried out for the Philippines case support this generalization. To isolate the separate characteristics of the trade reform, tariff reductions and a devaluation were first examined separately. The CGE model was run to approximate full compliance with the tariff reductions and export promotion reforms required by structural adjustment. In the resulting estimates production, income distribution, and the balance of payments all improve over their benchmark levels, though employment declines. *(See Table 5.4.)* The prices of capital and land rise relative to wages. The environmental implications of tariff reform are generally adverse. Erosion-prone farming of maize and rootcrops expands by 2.5 percent, though agricultural land also shifts into production of rice, coffee, and coconut, which are less erosive crops. Logging, fishing, and mining also increase. Because the domestic price of

Table 5-4. Environmental Effects of Trade Reforms

	Trade Liberalization	Devaluation by 20%	Joint Reform	Environmental Implications
	Percent Change from Base Case			
Sectors:				
Real GDP	+2.30	−0.15	+2.43	Positive income effects
Erosion-Prone Agriculture	+2.49	−0.47	+2.45	Increased soil erosion
Logging	+1.33	+0.24	+7.25	Promoted deforestation
Fishery	+.13	−0.20	+0.44	Marginal increase in fishery exploitation
Mining	+27.83	+0.39	+29.38	Promoted depletion
Energy	+4.76	+0.02	+3.00	Increased energy use
General Indicators: Change in Price of:				
Labor	Negative	Positive	Negative	Increased migration pressure
Land	Positive	Negative	Positive	to marginal resources and
Capital	Positive	Negative	Positive	demand for land in traded goods sectors
BOP:	Positive	Positive	Positive	
Income Distribution	Positive	Positive	Positive	Positive income effects

Notes: 1. These are long-run effects relative to a "NO REFORM" increase that approximates the economic conditions of the early 1980s.

2. Erosion-prone agriculture includes corn and rootcrops sectors; mining refers to metallic ores.

imported crude oil declines, energy use expands by nearly 5 percent.

A 20 percent devaluation was then simulated to estimate the effect of establishing equilibrium in the foreign exchange market. As expected, this reform improves the balance of payments, but real GDP declines marginally. Since this income decline affects richer households more heavily, income distribution improves. Because devaluation promotes labor-intensive activities, wages increase relative to the prices of capital and land. Mining output increases 39 percent in response to the devaluation. The fishing sector contracts because of higher fuel costs for fishing vessels, but logging increases in response to higher export prices in pesos. The area under erosive upland crops declines. Thus, the net impact of devaluation on soil erosion is uncertain.

When taken together, tariff reduction and devaluation lead to real GDP growth, better income distribution, and balance-of-payments improvements, as expected by the framers of the structural adjustment program. In actual experience, the effects of tariff cuts dominated, since tariffs were cut but devaluation was undermined by domestic inflation. Accordingly, the program as implemented could have been expected to have adverse environmental consequences through sectoral shifts in production.

Clearly, more active promotion of labor-using industry together with countervailing efforts to strengthen environmental protection and resource management should have been key components of an environmentally sensitive adjustment program.

The sectoral environmental consequences— had the joint reforms been undertaken—would have been mostly detrimental, according to this simulation. Both logging and mining expand dramatically, by 7.3 percent and 29.4 percent, respectively. Energy use grows by 3.0 percent, and erosion-prone agriculture increases by 2.5 percent. Fishing also marginally increases. These results show that if the reforms were fully implemented and the original goals had been achieved, resource-based exports and environmentally damaging production sectors would have expanded. Since no safeguards or structural reforms were included in the programs to counter these heightened environmental pressures, resource degradation would almost certainly have intensified. Clearly, more active promotion of labor-using industry together with countervailing efforts to strengthen environmental protection and resource management should have been key

components of an environmentally sensitive adjustment program.

2. Industrial Promotion

Industrial incentives are incorporated in the CGE model by increasing the returns to capital in preferred sectors relative to 1979 levels to reflect the adjustment program's industry-specific incentives. These incentive changes, expressed as reductions in capital costs, were weighted depending on each industry's importance to output in a particular sector. Although the purpose of the reform of industrial incentives was to replace capital-cheapening incentives with performance-oriented measures, the industrial incentive program after adjustment still reduced capital costs differentially (Pante and Medalla, 1990).

The simulation demonstrates that although the incentives are intended to encourage industrial growth and exports, neither increases much. Manufacturing grows by only 0.2 percent and exports by even less. *(See Table 5.4.)* While industrial incentives increased investment and output in the preferred sectors, these gains were offset by reductions in investment and production in other sectors. The net macroeconomic effect was scarcely improved aggregate output. The total effect on employment is also marginal, and the reform would have further skewed the distribution of income. In addition, the environmental effects are all negative. Erosion, deforestation, over-fishing, mineral depletion, and energy use all increase marginally. These results suggest that such industrial investment incentives are ineffective at best, and counterproductive at worst. The government's limited resources and program implementation capabilities would have been better employed in other ways.

3. Energy Reforms

The model's energy sector sub-model does not discriminate between increases in electricity prices and in oil prices. The focal point of energy policy reforms was electricity rates, which previously fell below long-run marginal cost by about 30 percent. The government's National Power Corporation generates almost all electricity. Since electricity and petroleum are the two largest energy sources, an electricity price increase can be simulated conservatively by an additional 10-percent indirect tax on the whole sector.

Real GDP declines by 0.5 percent in the model as the result of the energy price increase, though balance-of-payments effects are beneficial. *(See Table 5.5.)* Production becomes more labor-intensive, but because of the energy sector's extensive links to commercial activities, all producing sectors contract, including agriculture, forestry, fishing, energy, and mining activities that contribute to environmental degradation. These results suggest that efforts to increase power rates promote conservation not only in the energy sector itself but also in other degradation-prone sectors. From the environmental as well as the economic perspective, energy price increases represent a comparatively appealing revenue source in the Philippines.

C. Elements of an Alternative Program

The preceding simulations suggest that macroeconomic policy changes have broad and significant effects on the environment. Designing environmental considerations into structural adjustment programs could therefore alter the fundamental patterns of environmental degradation discussed in Parts II–IV: natural resource disinvestment, increasing input use, industrial pollution, and population pressure on marginal resources due to underemployment.

Modifying these patterns requires managing some difficult trade-offs. To reduce pressures on marginal resources, income and employment elsewhere in the economy must increase, at the risk of greater pollution and resource degradation. Therefore, governments must establish mechanisms to control environmental damages and to minimize the dependence of the economy on such degradation-prone sectors as logging, mining, and upland cropping. Sectors that have significant productivity and employment potential, such as lowland agriculture and tree cropping, present more environmentally benign sources of growth. Policies to stimulate these sectors are preferable on economic and environmental grounds to the usual capital-cheapening incentives for pollution-prone industries. As our assessments have shown, industrial promotion and import-substitution incentives are not very useful anyway.

Trade liberalization may have damaging environmental consequences that undermine its contribution to sustainable development, especially if environmental and resource controls are not strengthened through policy and institutional reforms.

Trade liberalization may have damaging environmental consequences that undermine its contribution to sustainable development, especially if environmental and resource controls are not strengthened through policy and institutional reforms. Resource rent taxes and environmental charges are examples of countervailing instruments that should be incorporated into the adjustment program to alleviate or reverse the environmental effects of adjustment programs, while mobilizing resources, promoting efficiency, and reducing inequities. Changes in land tenure and property rights are institutional reforms that can, by giving households a more secure stake in resource management, mitigate rural environmental degradation associated with structural adjustment and contribute to other economic goals as well.

Table 5-5. Environmental Effects of Energy Taxation and Industrial Promotion

	Percent Change from Base Case		
	10% Energy Tax	Industrial Subsidy	Environmental Implications
Sectors:			
Real GDP	−0.54	+0.06	Energy taxation constrains economy growth.
Erosion-prone Agriculture	−0.72	+0.17	Industrial subsidies generally stimulate sectors prone to environmental degradation.
Logging	−0.09	−0.05	
Fishing	−0.83	−0.07	Energy taxes reduce resource exploitation.
Mining	−0.08	+0.64	
Energy	−3.86	+0.01	
General Indicators:			
Change in Price of:			
Labor	Negative	Positive	Energy taxes reduce demand for land, labor, and capital.
Land	Negative	Positive	
Capital	Negative	Positive	
Effect on:			
Balance-of-payments	Positive	Negative	Balance-of-payments improves due to decreased domestic demand.
Income Distribution	Positive	Negative	

Notes: 1. These are long-run effects relative to a "NO REFORM" increase that approximates the economic conditions of the early 1980s.

2. Erosion-prone agriculture includes corn and rootcrops sectors; mining refers to metallic ores.

3. The energy tax is specified as an indirect tax on energy output. *See* text for specification of industrial incentives.

Two sets of reforms that constitute the elements of an alternative program are analyzed below.

1. Fiscal Reforms and Domestic Resource Mobilization

Philippine taxes have been low but regressive. In the past decade, tax revenues annually amounted to less than 10 percent of GDP, and indirect taxes contribute more than 70 percent of tax revenue. Poorer households pay more relative to their incomes than families that are better off. In the Philippines, real estate taxes, mostly by local governments, have historically contributed less than 1 percent of total tax revenues (Habito, 1990). Clearly, an increase in direct taxes on income and property would make the revenue structure fairer.

Although tax reforms were not emphasized in the early structural adjustment loans, the economic recovery program (1987) introduced valued-added taxation (VAT) in the Philippines. The VAT system replaced turnover taxes for manufacturers, millers, brokers, and lessors of personal property and business assets. The VAT rate was 10 percent on the sale or importation of most goods, though a long list of exports and agricultural goods was exempt. The objectives of the change in tax structure were to reduce large variations in the taxation of inputs, to increase revenues, to simplify tax administration, and to reduce regressivity. A recent study using a CGE model similar to that used here showed that, because of its many exemptions, revenues would diminish when the VAT system was adopted. The tax burden was also made only marginally more progressive. Thus, the VAT program did not address the basic problem of poor tax yields and regressive tax incidence (Habito and Manasan, 1990).

A broad program of direct (resource and land) taxation can mobilize resources and promote resource conservation. Ideally, resource taxation should capture all surplus earnings. For example, current studies in forestry indicate that up to 60 percent of timber concessionaires' profits could be appropriated, still leaving sufficient earnings to cover standard margins for profit and risk. To examine the implications of resource taxes in forestry and metal mining, taxes set at 60 percent of capital income were introduced into the CGE model.

Resource taxes marginally decrease real GDP, but improve the balance of payments. *(See Table 5.6.)* The distribution of income also improves since capital returns normally go only to richer households. Employment rises, while capital and land use decline. Logging and mining activity falls off dramatically. The model predicts then, that resource taxes represent a revenue source that could reduce environmental degradation and alleviate poverty.

Environmental controls are modelled in the form of environmental charges designed to reduce the externalities associated with degradation-prone activities. In this model, associating the taxes directly with emissions or ecological damages was not possible. Unlike rent taxes, environmental taxes are levied on specific units of output, reflecting the environmental losses associated with that production process. Since the tax will alter product price, both the producer and the buyer pay the environmental cost. In addition, the tax creates incentives to reduce the output of such products (Baumol and Oates, 1988).

To simulate environmental taxation as a response to the soil erosion associated with logging, the model was run with a tax of 20 percent charged on the output of the logging sector. The tax rate approximates the environmental fee of about $500 per hectare logged that the government has imposed. The results show a 26-percent relative price increase for logs and a 4.5-percent drop of real output in the sector. The higher output price reflects the environmental cost associated with logging, and the lower output conforms to the expected conservation effect of externality taxes. Economy-wide effects are limited: forestry employment declines by 0.5 percent, forestry exports

Table 5-6. Environmental Effects of Resource Rent Taxation

Sectors:	Percent Change from Base Case with 60% Rent Tax on Logging and Mining	Environmental Implications
Real GDP	−0.19	Aggregate output declines marginally.
Erosion-Prone Agriculture	−0.09	Erosion-prone agriculture shrinks marginally.
Logging	−4.48	Substantial declines in resource exploitation.
Fishing	−0.41	
Mining	−2.34	
Energy	−0.22	
General Indicators:		
Change in Price of:		
Labor	Positive	
Land	Negative	Reduced pressure on land resources.
Capital	Negative	
Effects of:		
Balance-of-Payments	Positive	Both balance-of-payments and income distribution improves.
Income Distribution	Positive	

increase by 0.2 percent, and overall GDP goes down by 0.2 percent. However, income distribution improves as total employment increases and land and capital use decline.

These tax policy simulations indicate that a combination of resource rent and environmental taxes can reduce resource degradation while increasing government revenues (decreased budget deficits) and improving income distribution. In tandem with the growth-oriented structural adjustment programs, these tax approaches provide a workable alternative to the limited fiscal sector adjustments carried out in the Philippines.

2. Environment- and Growth-oriented Reforms

Land reform and support for smallholder lowland agriculture would promote productivity, equity, and resource conservation. It would radically change the rewards of land ownership and household saving and investment behavior. In the model used here, land reform is simulated by a combination of structural and behavioral changes. First, a third of the income from land accruing to the top income group is redistributed to the lowest income group of households, and the savings rate of the recipient group is raised from 0 to 1 percent of income. (The land reform was assumed to apply to land under all crops.)

Both output and employment in the model increase under the assumption of land reform, as does agricultural and fisheries production. Manufacturing sector output also expands in response to the increase in consumer demand. Income distribution improves markedly:

incomes of the poor rise by 14 percent while those of the rich fall by 5 percent. Land prices rise relative to other factor costs. Land shifts into lowland crop production, not into erosion-prone crops or timber production. Energy use rises marginally.

Institutional and policy changes such as these, designed to provide incentives for better environmental and resource management, complement the more standard sectoral incentive programs previously described. Their effect will be to reduce substantially the environmental damages associated with adjustment programs.

Conclusions

Adjustment for Sustainable Development

The focus of macroeconomic policies in the Third World must extend beyond the immediate crises and encompass longer-term goals of sustainable development. At present, stabilization programs do not. Structural adjustment programs, even though they are intended to create an appropriate policy framework for long-term growth, also omit crucial environmental safeguards. Macroeconomic policies determine patterns of production, trade, investment, and income distribution. For good or ill, they therefore inevitably also influence how natural resources and the environment are used.

Policies that depress savings and lower the returns to investment shift resource use toward the present. Unmanageable domestic and external indebtedness are widely observable symptoms of this intertemporal reallocation. Less scrutinized but even more serious has been the depletion of natural resource assets. And yet, the analysis of the Philippines experience demonstrates that the rise in external debt and the depletion of natural wealth are both part of a general deterioration in the national balance sheet. They both arise from short-sighted policies. To promote sustainable development, macroeconomic policies must provide strong incentives to build capital—not just financial and industrial capital, but also natural resource and human capital. The deterioration of a nation's natural resource endowment is at least as serious an obstacle to sustainable development as the deterioration of its international credit standing.

The rise in external debt and the depletion of natural wealth are both part of a general deterioration in the national balance sheet. They both arise from short-sighted policies.

Reallocation of productive resources among sectors to achieve greater efficiency is the essence of structural adjustment programs. Changes in market incentives through reform of trade regimes, domestic price structures, taxes, and subsidies are the policy instruments of reallocation. However, if full environmental and resource costs are not reflected in the incentives resource users face, then efficiency will not be achieved either in the short or the long run. The Philippines study shows that macroeconomic policies without adequate environmental controls have increased emissions, concentrated pollution and congestion, increased pressure on open-access resources, and encouraged overexploitation of depletable resources. Structural adjustment policies have been designed without adequate consideration of such effects and implemented without the safeguards and corrective policies needed to control and reduce adverse environmental impacts. Without these intrinsic environmental components, there is no assurance that they effectively promote sustainable development.

Structural adjustment policies have been designed without adequate consideration of ecological effects and implemented without the safeguards and corrective policies needed to control and reduce adverse environmental impacts. Without these intrinsic environmental components, there is no assurance that they effectively promote sustainable development.

Such safeguards should not be regarded as impediments to structural adjustment policies or burdensome concessions to environmental interest groups. Indeed, policy and institutional reforms to correct environmental failures are complementary and essential components of a structural adjustment program. Policies can readily be identified that reduce environmental damage and simultaneously promote other economic objectives, such as fiscal balance, poverty alleviation, and economic efficiency. The Philippines study identifies several important examples, such as the taxation of resource rents, energy taxes, and the elimination of industrial incentives.

Recognizing the role of macroeconomic policies in environmental decline is the critical first step in formulating such an alternative approach. The World Bank and the IMF, as the main proponents and supporters of macroeconomic policy reform in the developing world, should actively promote new analytical approaches that simultaneously address structural reform and environmental needs. These institutions should have the capabilities and resources needed to carry out studies such as this one, with far greater sophistication and thoroughness, in cooperation with all of their clients.

Environmental organizations should also recognize that they need to extend their scrutiny and advocacy beyond their traditional concerns with individual investment projects and sectoral policies. They will have to take positions on national economic policy and structural reform programs. Those positions should be based on a deeper understanding of the direct and indirect workings of macroeconomic policies, not on oversimplifications and overgeneralizations regarding complex issues. This is a challenge to become involved, not an excuse to stand aside.

Wilfrido Cruz was an associate at WRI while completing this report. He was project manager of this Philippine macroeconomics and sustainable development study and of the Costa Rica natural resource accounting study. He is currently with the Environment Department of the World Bank. **Robert Repetto** is Vice President and Senior Economist at WRI and Director of the Institute's Program in Economics and Population.

Appendix 2.1 Resource Accounting Methodology for the Forestry Sector[67]

T his appendix describes in detail the derivation of the forestry accounts in Table 2.8.

Physical Accounts

Physical stocks and any change in timber resources during an accounting period can be recorded in physical units. The accounting principle is that opening stocks plus all growth or addition (reforestation) minus all extraction (harvesting), natural degradation (fire, insect, infestations, etc.), or deforestation (conversion of land use) equal closing stocks.[68] In the physical accounts, timber resources are expressed in hectares or in cubic meters. Since this study focuses on commercially productive forests, only virgin (old growth) and secondary (young growth) dipterocarp forests were included in the timber resource accounts. It also should be noted that logging converts virgin forest to secondary forest without changing total forest areas; deforestation occurs when secondary forest lands are converted to other uses.

Growing Stock. To estimate areas of physical growing timber stock, the two forest inventory data sets available for the Philippines are used. *(See Table 2.8.)* The area for 1970 in the accounts was based on the First Inventory, which was completed in 1969. The 1987 area was based on the second inventory. The 1987 assessment is cited by the World Bank (1989b) as the most accurate data set. Areas for the remaining years were computed as a straight line between the two benchmark years.

Because the inventory data for dipterocarp forests are not broken down into old and secondary growth areas, their proportions are derived from separate estimates reported in the 1987 Philippine Forestry Statistics. For example, in 1987, the DENR reported that of the 4,839 thousand hectares of dipterocarp forest, 1,220 thousand hectares (or 25.21 percent) were old growth while 3,619 thousand hectares were secondary growth. Thus, the 4,330 thousand hectares of total dipterocarp forest from Table 2.8 were multiplied by 0.2521 to derive the estimate of old growth area. The balance was assumed to be secondary growth area.

The measure of stocking volume used is "volume over bark" (VOB): "gross volume in cubic meter (c.m.) per hectare over bark of free bole (from stump or buttresses to crown point of first main branch) of all living trees more than 10 centimeters in diameter at breast height."[69] This study uses the regional VOB values obtained in the FAO study in 1981. Stocking rate estimates in the Philippines by the FAO are 309m^3/ha for old growth forests and 165m^3/ha for young growth forest. These stocking rate estimates were applied to the estimated old growth forest areas.

Tree plantation production was not included in the accounts because plantations were either unproductive or did not generate significant resource rents.

Growth and Reproduction. An annual increment in volume of all trees in the forest can be expected only from the secondary forests, since virgin forest is assumed to have reached its climax growth level.[70] This study assumes an estimate of annual growth increment of young dipterocarp forests at 1.3 m³/ha/year,[71] based on the Forestry Masterplan assessments.

Harvesting. The volume of the total log harvest was reported by the Forest Management Bureau in the 1988 Philippines Statistical Yearbook. As is the case in Indonesia, these figures may be underestimated due in part to illegal logging and under-invoicing of exports, both intended to avoid export restrictions, taxes, and royalties. The reported log harvest peaked in 1975 and then gradually declined, largely because commercially valuable, as well as physically and legally accessible, timber resources had become increasingly scarce. The figures on the reported harvest were used directly in the physical accounts.

Deforestation and Degradation. Deforestation refers to the conversion of forest lands to other uses. Shifting and permanent cultivation, reservoirs, and other infrastructure are considered to be the main causes of the shrinkage of forest areas. Deforestation in the Philippines has been substantial; it is reported that 18 million people—equivalent to almost one third of the total Philippine population—live in the upland forests.[72] Many of these millions are landless shifting cultivators who settle in logged forests.

The deforestation rate of 176,000 hectares per year (from Table 2.7) was multiplied by the second growth stocking rate (165m³/ha) to determine volume lost due to deforestation.

"Degradation refers to forest deterioration due to such natural disasters as fires, earthquakes, and pests, and due to destructive exploitation of forest resources by logging operations, grazing, and fuelwood collection."[73] Logging damage occurs during logging operations largely because most loggers have no economic incentive to protect residual trees.

Repetto et al. (1989) used a damage estimate of 1.9m³ for each cubic meter logged. This is based on studies that 40 percent of residual trees are damaged after logging. Estimates of damage to residual trees are smaller in the Philippines. A current study by a natural resource accounting project of the DENR proposed a significantly lower damage estimate of 0.8m³ per cubic meter logged. (Delos Angeles, personal communication, March 1991). This is the rate used in Table 2.7.

Fires are an important factor in forest destruction. Forest fires occur mostly in logged-over forest as dead trees and branches ignite during dry seasons. DENR Forestry statistics report fire-affected areas for 1980–87. This study employs mortality rates in the burned area at 25 percent as estimated in the Indonesian case study.[74] This mortality rate sets the loss at 41.25 m³ per hectare affected by fire (165 x 0.25). The average fire damage in the seven years from 1980 to 1987 (excluding 1983, due to unusually large fire loss) is 9,070 ha per year uing the mortality rate of 41.25, and 0.37 m³ (41.25 x 0.009). An annual loss of 0.37 million m³ (41.25m³ x 9,070 ha) was used for the preceding 10 years, from 1970 to 1979, when data was not available.

Net Change and Closing Stock of Physical Account

The principal sources of addition to and reduction in forest resources are the categories above. Because the 1987 forest area data were considered the most accurate, the volume at the end of 1987 was first estimated using the FAO stocking volume for old and secondary growth forest. This yielded 871.65 million m³. The net volume losses from the additions and reductions computations were then used to work backward to derive stock estimates for every year from 1986 to 1970. The 1970 opening stock that results from this process, 1550.6 million m³, is significantly smaller than the 1970 opening stock computed using the 1970 forest inventory area multiplied by the FAO

Stocking volumes. The discrepancy is due primarily to the underestimates of logging and of the deforestation rate that were used. The account's net volume losses per year were thus probably smaller than actual losses, implying that the 1987 volume of 871.65 million m³ was reached from a relatively small starting stock in 1970.

The Value Accounts

Economic Rent and Monetary Accounts. The concept of economic rent is essential for natural resource valuation since it places monetary value on changes in physical assets. (Economic rent is the return to any production input over the minimum amount required to retain it in its present use.) In forest economics, economic rent can be estimated by timber "stumpage value," the market value of the standing timber prior to any value added by processing. Therefore, the economic rent of timber is equivalent to the net price determined by the world timber price less all factor costs incurred in extraction, including a normal return to capital but excluding taxes, duties, and royalties.[75]

To estimate the value of natural resource stocks, Landefeld and Hines (1985) compared, using the present value of pure net revenues, the transaction value of market purchases, the sales of the resource *in situ*, and the net price or unit rent of the resource multiplied by the relevant quantity of the reserve. While the present value method requires complicated information—estimates of prices, operating costs, production levels, and interest rates over the life of forest resources—the net price method requires only current data on prices and costs. However, with equilibrium in resource markets, depletion as measured by changes in the present value of the resource equals depletion as measured by the net price method. (Landefeld and Hines, 1985). Thus the current economic rent per unit of a resource product can be used as the approximation of the present value of the product's expected future net income.

The export value has been measured directly by the free on board (f.o.b.) export unit value in current dollars, which is the ratio between gross export revenue and volume of log exports. This estimate of timber value is conservative since log exports have been considerably under-invoiced due to avoidance of export taxes and log smuggling, especially after the log export ban started in 1985.[76] Because the export prices in 1986 and 1987 are not reliable, due to possible price distortion from log export ban, the prices for those years were calculated based on the f.o.b. values for Malaysia in the same years, by taking the price ratio between the two countries in the preceding years.

Transportation and log extraction costs are considered to be the main logging costs. The average production cost per cubic meter of log from 1979–83 were based on Boado's (1988) estimates. The figures for the other years in Table 2.8 were computed according to f.o.b. export prices and the average unit cost/price ratio in the five years, by assuming that the same relation between unit cost and price held for the other years. Average stumpage value or potential primary rents per m³ for logs actually harvested was calculated by deducting these production cost estimates from the respective f.o.b. export unit value. In the base year 1979, for example, this method yielded a potential primary rent of $69/m³ from a f.o.b. unit value of $116, less a production cost of $47. These calculations produced average unit rents equal to 52 percent of f.o.b. unit value, which is very similar to the figures of 53 to 55 percent calculated in the Indonesian case study.[77]

Since mature virgin forest stands are commercially much more valuable than young growth forest stands, potential rents for secondary forests are lower. The assessment in Repetto et al. (1989) that secondary rent is one-half of primary rent is used in these accounts. The actual net price applied to the physical net charge measures is an average of the rent estimates at the start of the year and at the end. The primary rent is used for log harvests, and the secondary rent is used for all other charges.

Appendix 5.1 Profile of Structural Adjustment Loans

I. SAL I

Program Description

Scope/Objectives: The Program aims to promote exports through improvements in the incentive system, liberalize the tariff structure and simplify import procedures, and restructure selected industries.

Implementation Schedule: 1980–1983

Program Financing

Funding Source: International Bank for Reconstruction and Development

Amount: US $200 Million

Terms: Interest on principal—9.24%
Commitment charge—0.75%
Repayment period—20 years (including 5 years grace)

Scope of Financing: Import of industrial raw materials, intermediate goods, capital goods, spare parts and other goods.

Disbursement: Two tranches, the first upon loan effectiveness, the second when satisfactory progress is made in realigning tariffs and liberalizing import licensing.

Date of Loan Signing: 25 September 1980

Status: Fully disbursed. First tranche released in December 1980 and the second in July 1981.

Technical Assistance

Funding Source: International Bank for Reconstruction and Development

Amount: $5 Million

II. SAL II

Program Description

Scope/Objectives:

The structural adjustment program aims at improving the allocation and efficiency of investment over the medium term. The second phase of the program includes:

i) a fundamental reform of the Philippines' industrial incentives and promotion policy;

ii) an extension of the ongoing trade policy reform through measures in indirect taxation, import liberalization, and tariffs; and

iii) reforms in energy policy and public resource management.

The program also aims at improving the structure of the balance of payments by limiting the country's reliance on foreign savings and reducing the current account deficit to more sustainable levels.

Implementing Agency:

Inter-Agency Committee to Monitor and Coordinate the Structural Adjustment Program

Implementation Schedule: One year (1984)

Program Financing

Funding Source

International Bank for Reconstruction and Development

Amount:

US $302.3 Million

Terms:

Interest on principal—standard variable rate
Commitment charge—0.75%
Repayment period—20 years (including 5 years grace)

Scope of Financing:

Essential imports estimated at about 4% of Philippine merchandise imports and meet 8% of gross external capital requirements in 1983.

Disbursement:

Two tranches; $203.2 M upon loan effectiveness and the second tranche of $100 M after six (6) months, after a review of the progress made in implementing the program.

Date of Loan Signing:

27 April 1983.

Status:

Fully disbursed.

Appendix 5.2 A General Equilibrium Model for Resource Use Analysis

I. The Computable General Equilibrium Model

The use of a general equilibrium approach to modelling the impacts of exchange rate, tariff, and taxation changes captures the interactions between supply and demand, within the markets for agricultural goods, as well as between those markets and the rest of the economy. Thus, for example, changes in the exchange rate have been shown to affect the agricultural sector and changes in the agricultural sector have important impacts on the remainder of the economy (Habito, 1986).

The model constructed for this study follows in the tradition of the Shoven and Whalley tax-analysis research.[78] As such, it recognizes that consumers' preferences are a function of their incomes and specifies a distinct demand system for each group of households. Additionally, a neoclassical microeconomic model of producer behavior is employed. The model of consumer behavior is integrated with a model of producer behavior to provide a comprehensive framework for policy simulations.

The general equilibrium nature of the model is reflected by its goal of determining a vector of prices for consumer goods and services and of producer goods and services that will clear all markets. The equilibrium prices determine the optimal allocation of resources, given the endowments of labor, capital, and land.

On the production side, technologies are represented by production functions that exhibit constant elasticities of substitution (CES). Technological progress (both embodied and disembodied) is assumed not to occur over the period of investigation.

On the demand side, the model captures the behavior of consumers (who can also serve as investors), the government, and foreigners. Consumers are grouped according to income and a demand system is specified for each group. Each income group has an endowment of labor and capital and, given the vector of prices, decides the amount to save and invest and the amount of each good and service. Investment, consequently, is determined by savings. The government levies taxes on both production and consumption. That is, there are taxes on factors of production, on output, on income, and on consumption. Revenue is used to distribute income back to consumers and to purchase goods and services, as well as capital and labor. The foreign sector produces imports and consumes exports.

Table 1 details the specific producing sectors and types of consumer goods and services considered in the general equilibrium model. Three household categories (classified by income) are delineated in Table 2 and roughly divide all households into equal groups. This choice of the level of disaggregation was dictated by data availability and by the economic variables of interest.

Table 1. Classification of Producing Sectors and Consumer Goods and Services	
Industries	**Consumer Goods**
1. Manufacturing	1. Housing
2. Forestry	2. Transportation
3. Forest Products	3. Education
4. Rice	4. Milk and Meat
5. Corn	5. Alcohol and Tobacco
6. Root Crops	6. Cereals
7. Coconut	7. Fish
8. Services	8. Fuel
9. Metal Mining	9. Medical Services
10. Nonmetal Mining	10. Household Services
11. Energy	11. Clothing
12. Fisheries	12. Other Processed Food
13. Coffee	13. Misc. Food Items
14. Sugar and Misc. Crops	14. Misc. Goods

Table 2. Household Categories Based on Income	
Category	**Income Range (Phil. Pesos)**
1	0–14,999
2	15,000–29,999
3	30,000 and over

II. The Model

A. Production

The production side is composed of an input-output model with some flexibility with regard to the substitution of factor inputs (capital, labor, and land). The degree of flexibility depends, of course, on the mathematical specification of the production function. In the current model, each production sector is assumed to have a constant elasticity of substitution: the value added by the specific sector is a function of labor and capital. For the agricultural and forestry sectors, however, a third factor of production, land, is included to allow an assessment of land-use changes from policy experiments.

Land factor is incorporated by nesting the CES production function. In particular, an input is defined that is solely a function (in CES form) of land and capital; this, in turn, takes the place of capital in the original production specification. While it would be possible to simply add land as an explicit input in the production function, doing so implicitly suggests that the elasticity of substitution between all pairs of inputs is the same. By nesting, however, the substitution elasticities are allowed to vary among inputs.

B. Demand

The output of the fourteen producing sectors accrues to the owners of the factors of production. With the receipts from these sales, these individuals consume domestic or foreign goods and services, save, or pay taxes to the government.

The demand for final goods and services comes from their primary sources. First, final goods and services may be directly consumed by individuals. Second, investment (which is equal to savings) consumes some of the goods and services produced.

A review of Table 1 will show that the composition of the consumer goods and services does not match that of the producing sectors because final goods and services must go through various channels (i.e., transportation and distribution) before they can be consumed. To address this problem, a transformation matrix defines the contribution of each producing sector to the consumption of each of the final (consumer) goods and services.

For each category of households (refer to Table 2), utility is assumed to be a weighted CES function of the 14 consumer goods and services. The weights on these goods (which are household category-specific) are computed as the share of total purchase going to a specific consumer good or service.

A household's budget constraint is defined so that expenditures on goods and services must be less than or equal to household income. In turn, income equals the returns to labor plus the returns to capital plus the returns to land. In other words, expenditures by a household must be less than or equal to the total factor payments it receives. Maximizing utility subject to this expenditure constraint leads to the estimate of the demand for the various goods and services by household categories. Observe that since savings is considered as one of the items on an individual's utility function, the choice between consumption and savings is explicit. That is, intertemporal tradeoffs are an integral part of the model.

The second component of demand for goods and services is investment. Like the final demand by individuals, total investment is disaggregated (through a transformation matrix) by the sector of the economy that produces it. Since savings are assumed to exactly equal investment (as given by the *Statistical Yearbook of the Philippines*), personal savings are scaled to equal the gross investment (measured) for each of the 14 producing sectors.

The final component of demand for goods and services is the demand by foreign consumers. In the model, exports (i.e., foreign demand) are delineated by the producing sector. That is, a transformation matrix analogous to the matrix used for the consumption of final goods and services is not used. A similar delineation is employed for imports (i.e., foreign supply). By employing both demand and supply elasticity estimates,[79] export-and-import demand relationships are constructed for each producing sector.

C. *Taxes and the Government*

For the purpose at hand, the government is treated as a separate sector with a CES utility function. (That is, it is treated in a fashion analogous to one of the household sectors.) The elasticity of substitution is assumed to be one. The government collects tax revenue in various forms. Taxes include the personal income tax, labor taxes (e.g., social security tax), capital taxes (e.g., a corporate income tax), property taxes, tariffs, and sales and excise taxes. All of the taxes are treated as *ad valorem* taxes and a marginal rate is used for each household.

With the tax revenues collected, the government produces public goods and redistributes income. Hence, all tax revenue is eventually returned to consumers as transfer payments or subsidies or as payments for capital or labor services (the two factors of production used by the government).

III. A Mathematical Statement of the Model

Given these foregoing considerations, it is useful to state precisely the conditions that the model being used here must satisfy for a general equilibrium to exist. First, there cannot be positive excess quantities demanded. That is,

$$(1) \sum_{j=1}^{m} a_{ij} M_j - E_i (p,Y) \geq 0 \text{ for c.s. } p_i \geq 0$$

where i (i = 1, 2, ..., n) denotes the consumer goods and services. Mj (j = 1, 2, ..., m) denotes the activity levels, aij, denotes the ijth element in the activity analysis matrix, Y denotes a vector of incomes for the k consumers, p denotes a vector of prices for the n consumer goods and services, and E_i denotes the excess demand for good or service i.

The notation c.s. implies that complementary slackness holds for each consumer good and service. That is, if the expression (for a specific good or service i) is multiplied by p_i, then the relationship will hold with equality.

The second requirement for general equilibrium is that the profits associated with a given activity are not positive. That is:

$$(2) - \sum_{i=1}^{n} a_{ij} P_i \geq 0 \text{ for c.s. } M_j \geq 0$$

Finally, all prices and activity levels must be non-negative. That is:

(3a) $P_i \geq 0$, $i = 1, 2, \ldots, n$

and:

(3b) $M_j \geq 0$, $j = 1, 2, \ldots, m$.

The model is solved for a general equilibrium using the iterative algorithm nominally referred to as the Sequence of Linear Complementary Problems (SLCP) developed by Mathiesen (1985).[80]

Notes

1. *World Bank Support for the Environment: A Progress Report.* Development Committee Report No. 22, (Washington, D.C.: The World Bank, September, 1989).

2. This average does not include the ICOR for 1984 to 1985, which was negative.

3. The model does not currently include quality distinctions among lands used for various crops.

4. Although forestry rent taxation reforms have been included as the centerpiece of a recent World Bank environmental sector loan, the broader role of resource taxation was not recognized as a necessary component of domestic resource mobilization measures.

5. As discussed in Part V, the implementation of trade reforms was undermined by the severe contraction of the Philippine economy in 1984.

6. The consultative group for the Philippines was formed in 1970 and chaired by the World Bank to coordinate external aid to the Philippines from 13 countries and from the World Bank, International Monetary Fund, Asian Development Bank, European Economic Community, Organization for Economic Cooperation and Development, and the United Nations Development Program.

7. World Bank, *Philippines: A Framework for Economic Recovery,* (Washington DC: The World Bank, 1987), p. 4.

8. *Philippine Statistical Yearbook* (1989). Data series on investment are based on expenditures classified by type of good, not sector. The industrial sector's ICOR is generally larger than that for the whole economy. The 1970–82 sectoral estimates presented above are based on data from special surveys. *See* Table 2.15 for derivation of ICOR.

9. Tan (1979) found that for manufacturing sub-sectors, high EPRs were positively related with an index of foreign exchange use intensity and negatively related with export orientation.

10. World Bank (1976), p. 193.

11. This is discussed in detail in the forestry resource section below. *See also* Table 2.9.

12. For a discussion of various approaches to constructing resource accounts, *see* H. Peskin and E. Lutz, ''A Survey of Resource and Environmental Accounting in Industrialized Countries,'' World Bank Environment Department, Working Paper No. 37, 1990.

13. Actual forested area is different from land officially classified as forest. The latter increased from less than one third to one

half of the total land area during the last two decades. The government classifies land as forest to keep hilly areas prone to soil erosion from being converted to agriculture. Lands with slopes of more than 18 percent are deemed unsuitable for farming and are kept in the public forest domain on the presumption that forestry is their only sustainable use.

14. Appendix 2.1 presents the detailed procedure for constructing these accounts.

15. In Indonesia, the erosion loss was based on the decline in net farm income associated with soil erosion. This loss amounts to 1%–10% of the value of rainfed crop output (Repetto et al., 1989, Table II.13).

16. The interest rate used is 10%.

17. These projects had long reservoir service life due to substantial dead storage capacity built into their original design. Thus, increased erosion can be absorbed for many years in the dead storage. However, it has been suggested that, from an *ex ante* project view, the additional construction cost for large sediment capacities should be charged to soil erosion (W. Cruz et al. 1988).

18. Irrigated rice areas are assumed to produce 73 percent of total rice production.

19. *Muro-ami* refers to a fishing method that employs swimmers with scare lines to encircle coral locations where fish aggregate. The lines are weighted with rocks, and as the rocks are pounded by the swimmers along the coral bottoms fish are driven into a net. This technique destroys coral. (*See also* Silvestre et al. 1989 for case study data of reef destruction.)

20. Using a discount rate of 10%.

21. Refer to Repetto et al., *Accounts Overdue*, for a detailed derivation of fishery depreciation in Costa Rica.

22. The GDP deflator in Table 2.9 was used to adjust values to 1972 prices.

23. The Metro Manila area includes the city of Manila and 13 adjoining cities and municipalities.

24. World Bank (1976), p. 315.

25. A survey of these programs is presented in DENR (1989b) and Delos Angeles and Lasmarias (1990).

26. *See* OECD (1991), *The State of the Environment*, Table 14, p. 189, for a listing of environmental effects of pollution-prone industries.

27. The nominal protection for a commodity is measured as the difference between its domestic and international price, expressed as a proportion of the international price. The official exchange rate is used to convert the international price into domestic currency. In contrast, the EPR takes into account how inputs of the commodity are also affected by government intervention. Thus, EPR is computed as the difference between the value added of the activity using domestic prices and value added using international prices, expressed as a proportion of value added using international prices.

28. These are 1974 EPRs from Tan (1979).

29. Bautista et al. (1979), p. 63.

30. World Bank (1982), p. 47.

31. The primacy ratio is defined as the ratio of population in the largest city to the population in the next three cities with at least 500,000 population.

32. Because no city in Thailand other than Bangkok has more than half a million population, the index was infinite.

33. Based on the long run marginal cost of power generation.

34. Table 2.3 shows a declining real effective exchange rate index for 1973–74 and 1979–82. A decrease in REER means that the local currency has appreciated.

35. These refer to lands that can be privatized.

36. An international survey of patterns of adoption of high-yielding rice varieties found that the greater the proportion of a country's agricultural area under irrigation, the greater was the proportion of cropped area planted to modern varieties (David and Otsuka, 1990).

37. Based on rice yield data from the *Philippine Statistical Yearbook*, various years.

38. In addition to the decline in real rice prices, Pingali and Moya (1989) point out that even in the best managed farms and in experiment stations, yields have stagnated or declined since the 1970s.

39. World Bank calculations in *The Challenge of Poverty* (1988) suggest that the increase in poverty incidence was not as large as this official estimate concludes.

40. ILO (1974); *see also* Table 4.5a.

41. A regression calculation quantifying this relationship yielded the equation:

$$\text{Net Migrants} = 37.59 + \underset{(0.02)}{0.05}\ (\text{GDP/capita}) - \underset{(1.31)}{3.03}\ (\text{Pov. Incidence}).$$

Standard errors are in parentheses; R square = .91; number of observations = 13.

42. Technically, open access resources are those to which property rights do not exist and which can therefore be freely exploited by anybody. Resources to which property rights are not enforced are conceptually distinct, but are exploited in much the same way.

43. This is the well-known open-access equilibrium result discussed in the literature on common property resources. Since in the lowlands, labor is at least paid its marginal product, open access resources with increasing population density eventually do not provide a better long-term alternative.

44. Refer to Table 2-4 in Part II.

45. Sicat (1986).

46. Based on the Suits index. This index of tax progressivity is derived from the tax burden curve and is analogous to the Gini coefficient derived from the Lorenz curve. The index ranges from 1 (for a perfectly progressive tax) to −1 (for a perfectly regressive tax). The index declined from −.05 to −.11 during this period.

47. From 1970 to 1987, the ratio of indirect tax to total tax ranged from .29 to .77. The situation was worse in the agricultural sector, where the range was .72 to .95.

48. Based on various surveys reported by Agabin et al. (1989).

49. The Anti-Usury Act of 1916 set interest ceilings on loans. Deposit ceilings were legislated in 1956. These limits were in effect until 1974, when the transition to liberalization started. Interest rates were freed up in 1981 (for long-term loans of four years or longer) and in 1983 for short-term loans. (Gochoco, 1989)

50. Studies of rice-farming communities (Ledesma 1982, David and Otsuka 1990) support the national data on increasing landlessness.

51. The upper limit for concession size is 100,000 hectares, though over-lapping

ownership of the logging companies allows individuals to control substantially more than this.

52. Miscellaneous other forest use permits are issued, but these use mostly the same lands and have been excluded from this profile of public land distribution.

53. *See* David W. Bromley and Michael M. Cernea, 1989, ''The Management of Common Property Natural Resources,'' World Bank Discussion Paper No. 57, for an overview of resource access issues and Owen Lynch and Kirk Talbott, 1988, ''Legal Responses to the Philippine Deforestation Crisis'' in *The Journal of International Law and Politics*, Vol. 20, for a specific discussion of the Philippine case.

54. World Bank (1976), Table 10.4, p. 260.

55. Refer to Table 2-4 in Part II.

56. Another outlet for excess labor that became important from the mid-1970s was contract work in the Middle East. The number of overseas workers, already growing because of unemployment and low wages during the late 1970s, increased even more during the crisis period (NCSB 1989).

57. *See*, for example, Grootaert and Kanbur (1990).

58. Two general reviews are Sebastian and Alicbusan (1989) and Hansen (1988). Case studies for Mexico, Thailand, and the Ivory Coast are being undertaken by the World Wildlife Fund and the London Environmental Economics Centre.

59. This discussion draws on the assessment in Montes, *Stabilization and Adjustment Policies and Programs* (Helsinki: WIDER, 1987).

60. World Bank (1988a), p. 137.

61. Appendix Table 5.1 summarizes the conditionalities and implementation of the two Structural Adjustment Loans. Appendix 5.1 describes these loans in detail.

62. The program target was to liberalize 960 imports by 1983. (Alburo and Shephard)

63. Refer to Table 3-4.

64. In 1982, there was even a short-lived effort, justified primarily on conservation grounds, to ban all log exports.

65. Except for oil, the banana sector was the only sector where export prices increased. This was due to the robust Japanese market for bananas.

66. The environmental implications of upland agriculture, logging, and over-fishing are discussed in detail in Part II. Mining impacts on downstream activities have been documented by Briones (1985). Energy resource use is analyzed in Part III.

67. Prepared by Fumiko Fukuoka and Wilfrido Cruz.

68. Repetto et al. (1989), p. 17.

69. Repetto et al., p. 29.

70. Ibid. p. 30.

71. DENR 1989a.

72. Ma. Concepcion Cruz, Imelda Zosa-Feranil, and Cristela Goce ''Population Pressure and Migration: Implications for Upland Development in the Philippines'' *Journal of Philippines Development* No. 26, Vol. XV, No. 1 1988.

73. Repetto et al., p. 32.

74. Repetto et al., p. 32.

75. Repetto et al., p. 19.

76. Patrick B. Durst, *Factors Influencing Discrepancies between Forest Products Trade*

Reports of the Philippines and Its Trade Partners (Laguna: UPLB College of Forestry, 1985). There has been a noticeable gap between official export statistics by the supplier governments and import statistics by the consumer governments. Since import tax on logs is not usually imposed, import statistics tend to be consistent with the actual volume of imports.

77. Repetto et al., p. 36.

78. *See*, for example, Shoven, J. and J. Whalley (1972), "A General Equilibrium Calculation of the Effects of Differential Taxation of Income from Capital in the U.S.," in *Journal of Public Economics*, 1:281–321.

79. Mostly from C.F. Habito (1984), *Equity and Efficiency Tradeoffs in Philippine Tax Policy Analysis: A General Equilibrium Approach*, Doctoral Dissertation, Harvard University.

80. Mathiesen (1955), "Computational Experience in Solving Equilibrium Models by a Sequence of Linear Complementarity Problems," in *Operations Research*, (33) 6:1225–1250.

References

Agabin, Meliza; Mario Lamberte; Mahar Mangahas; and Alcestia Abrera. 1989. "Integrative Report on the Informal Credit Markets in the Philippines." Philippine Institute for Development Studies Working Paper No. 89-10.

Alburo, Florian and Geoffrey Shepherd. 1991. "The Timing and Sequencing of a Trade Liberalization Policy: The Case of the Philippines." In *Liberalizing Foreign Trade: The Experience of Korea, The Philippines, and Singapore* (Vol. 2) ed. by Demetrias Papageorgiou, Michael Michaely and Armine M. Chaoksi. Washington, DC: The World Bank.

Addison, T. and Demery, L. 1988. *The Economics of Poverty under Structural Adjustment*. London: Overseas Development Institute.

Azarcon, Yolanda. 1990. *Public Investments in Irrigation in the Philippines*. A thesis presented to the Graduate School of Cornell University, Ithaca, New York.

Barlow, C., Jayasuriya, S. and E. Price. 1983. *Evaluating Technology for New Farming Systems: Case Studies from Philippine Rice Farms*. Los Banos, Philippines: International Rice Research Institute.

Baumol, W. and W. Oates. 1988. *The Theory of Environmental Policy*. Englewood Cliffs, NJ: Prentice Hall.

Bautista, Romeo M. and John H. Power and Associates. 1979. *Industrial Promotion Policies in the Philippines*. Manila: Philippine Institute for Development Studies.

Blejer, Mario I. and Isabel Guerrero. 1990. "The Impact of Macroeconomic Policies on Income Distribution: An Empirical Study of the Philippines." In *Review of Economics and Statistics*. Vol LXXII, No. 3, August, pp. 414–423.

Boado, Eufresina L. 1988. "Incentive Policies and Forest Use in the Philippines." in Robert Repetto and Malcolm Gillis (eds.), *Public Policies and the Misuse of Forest Resources*, World Resources Institute, Cambridge University Press, New York: 165–205.

Boyce, James K. and Luyba Zarsky. 1988. "Capital Flight from the Philippines, 1962–1986." In *Journal of Philippine Development*, Vol. 15, No. 2, pp. 191–221.

Briones, Nicomedes. 1986. "Estimating Erosion Costs: A Philippine Case Study in the Lower Agno River Watershed." In Easter, William, John Dixon, and Maynard Hufschmidt (eds.) 1986. *Watershed Resources Management: An Integrated Framework with Studies from Asia and the Pacific*. (Boulder, CO: Westview Press.)

Bureau of Forestry Development. 1985. *Philippine Forestry Statistics*. Manila: Department of Environment and Natural Resources.

Cabanilla, L.S. 1990. "Government Must Promote Transport." In *Economic Notes*. Los

Banos, Philippines: Research and Training Program on Agricultural Policy.

Cornia, G.A., et al. (eds.). 1987. *Adjustment with a Human Face. Vol. 1. Protecting the Vulnerable and Promoting Growth.* (Oxford: Clarendon Press).

Cruz, C.J.; I. Zosa-Feranil; and C.L. Goce. 1988. ''Population Pressure and Migration: Implications for Upland Development in the Philippines.'' In *Journal of Philippine Development.* Vol. XV:26, No. 1, pp. 15–46.

Cruz, Ma. Concepcion, Imelda Zosa-Feranil, and Cristela Goce. 1986. ''Population Pressure and Migration: Implications for Upland Development in the Philippines.'' Working Paper No. 86-07, Center for Policy and Development Studies, University of the Philippines at Los Banos.

Cruz, Ma. Concepcion. 1991. ''Population Pressure, Economic Stagnation, and Deforestation in the Philippines.'' Report submitted to the World Resources Institute.

Cruz, Wilfrido, Herminia Francisco, and Zenaida Conway. 1988. ''The On-site and Downstream Costs of Soil Erosion in the Magat and Pantabangan Watersheds.'' In *Journal of Philippine Development.* Vol. XV, No. 1, pp. 85–112.

David, Wilfredo P. 1988. ''Soil and Water Conservation Planning: Policy Issues and Recommendations.'' *In Journal of Philippine Development.* Vol. XV, No. 1, pp. 47–84.

David, Cristina C., Wilfrido Cruz, et al. 1986. *Agenda for Action for the Philippine Rural Sector.* Manila: Philippine Institute for Development Studies and University of the Philippines at Los Banos.

David, Cristina C., R. Barker and A. Palacpac. 1984. ''Productivity in Philippine Agriculture.'' Discussion paper, Department of Agricultural Economics, International Rice Research Institute.

David, Cristina C. and Otsuka Otsuka. 1990. ''The Modern Seed-Fertilizer Technology and Adoption of Labor-Saving Technologies: The Philippine Case.'' Paper presented at the final workshop on the Differential Impact of the Modern Rice Technology Across Production Environments, International Rice Research Institute, Los Banos, Philippines, March 26–28.

David, Cristina C. 1983. ''Economic Policies and Philippine Agriculture.'' Working Paper Series No. 83-02, Philippine Institute for Development Studies.

De Dios, E.S., (ed.). 1984. *An Analysis of the Philippine Economic Crisis.* Quezon City, Philippines: University of the Philippines Press.

Delos Angeles, M.S., and N.C. Lasmarias. 1990. ''A Review of Philippine Natural Resource and Environmental Management 1986–1988.'' Working Paper Series No. 90-08, Philippine Institute for Development Studies.

Department of Agriculture. 1988. *Development Indicators in Philippine Agriculture.* Quezon City: Department of Agriculture.

Department of Environment and Natural Resources (DENR). 1989a. ''The Sustainable Forest Management Plan.'' In *Forestry Masterplan,* Quezon City, Philippines: Department of Environment and Natural Resources.

Department of Environment and Natural Resources (DENR). 1989b. *Philippine Strategy for Sustainable Development.* Quezon City, Philippines: Department of Environment and Natural Resources.

Department of Environment and Natural Resources (DENR). 1986 and 1988. *Philippine Forestry Statistics.* Quezon City, Philippines: Bureau of Forestry Development.

Department of Local Government and Community Development. 1985. Barangay Census.

Unpublished data from the Department of Local Government and Community Development.

Fischer, Stanley. 1986. "Issues in Medium-Term Macroeconomic Adjustment" In *The World Bank Research Observer*, 1: 163–82, July.

Fischer, Stanley and William Easterly. 1990. "The Economics of the Government Budget Constraints." In *The World Bank Research Observer*, Vol. 5, No. 2 (July).

Food and Agriculture Organization. 1981. *Tropical Forest Resources Assessment Project: Forest Resources of Tropical Asia*. Rome: Food and Agriculture Organization.

Food and Agriculture Organization. 1983. *Yearbook of Forest Products*. Rome: Food and Agriculture Organization.

Food and Agriculture Organization. 1984. *Land, Food and People*. Rome: Food and Agriculture Organization.

Food and Agriculture Organization. 1985. "Forest Resources of Tropical Africa." In *Technical Report of the Forest Resources Assessment Project*. Rome: Food and Agriculture Organization.

Gohoco, Socorro. 1989. "Financial Liberalization and Interest Rate Determination: The Case of the Philippines." Philippine Institute for Development Studies Working Paper No. 89-06.

Gomez, E.D. 1980. "Status Report on Research and Degradation Problems of the Coral Reefs of the East Asian Seas." South China Seas Fisheries Development and Coordinating Programme, Food and Agriculture Organization, UNEP/WG, 41/INF. 15, 66pp.

Grootaert, Christian, and Ravi Kanbur. 1990. "Policy-Oriented Analysis of Poverty and the Social Dimensions of Structural Adjustment: A Methodology and Proposed Application to Cote d'Ivoire, 1985-88." World Bank Social Dimensions of Adjustment Working Paper No. 1.

Habito, Cielito F. 1984. *Equity and Efficiency Tradeoffs in Philippine Tax Policy Analysis: A General Equilibrium Approach,* Doctoral Dissertation, Harvard University.

Habito, Cielito F.. 1986. "A General Equilibrium Model for Philippine Agricultural Policy Analysis. In *Journal of Philippine Development*. Vol. XIII, No. 23.

Habito, Cielito F. 1990. *Fiscal Policies in Philippine Agriculture*. Monograph No. 90-01, University of the Philippines Agricultural Policy Research Program, Los Banos, Philippines.

Habito, Cielito F. and Manasan, Rosario G. 1990. *Agricultural Taxation: A Case Study of the Philippines*. Manila: Philippine Institute for Development Studies.

Hansen, Stein. 1988. "Structural Adjustment Programs and Sustainable Development." Paper commissioned by the United Nations Environment Programme for the annual session of the Committee of International Development Institutions on the Environment, Washington, DC, June 13–17, 1988.

Hayami, Y., David, C.C., Flores, P. and Kikuchi, M. 1976. "Agricultural Growth Against a Land Resource Constraint: The Philippine Experience." In *Australian Journal of Agricultural Economics*, 20(3), 144–159.

Heller, P.S. et al. 1988. "The Implications of Fund-Supported Adjustment Programs for Poverty: Experiences in Selected Countries." Occasional Paper No. 58, International Monetary Fund, Washington, DC.

Hermosa, V.P., C.W. Paderanga and Associates. 1983. *The Spatial and Urban Dimensions of Development in the Philippines*. Manila: Philippine Institute for Development Studies.

Hooley, Richard. 1985. *Productivity Growth in Philippine Manufacturing: Retrospect and Future Prospects*. Manila: Philippine Institute for Development Studies.

Intal Jr., Ponciano S. and Pante, Jr., Filologo. 1989. "Can the Philippines Grow Out of Debt?" Paper presented at the Bangkok Conference on the Future of the Asia-Pacific Economies, Bangkok, Thailand, November 8–10.

Intal, P. and J. Power. 1990. *Trade, Exchange Rate, and Agricultural Pricing Policies in the Philippines*. Washington, DC: The World Bank.

Intal Jr., Ponciano S. and Pante, Jr., Filologo. 1989. "Can the Philippines Grow Out of Debt?" Paper presented at the Bangkok Conference on the Future of the Asia-Pacific Economies, Bangkok, Thailand, November 8–10.

Intal Jr., Ponciano S., Cristina C. David, and Gerald Nelson. 1987. "Philippine Economic Policies and Agricultural Development: A Review and an Agenda for the Future. " In Center for Policy and Development Studies, *Policy Issues on the Philippine Rice Economy and Agricultural Trade*. Los Banos, Philippines: University of the Philippines at Los Banos.

International Labor Office (ILO), 1974. *Sharing in Development: A Program of Employment Equity and Growth for the Philippines*, Geneva: International Labor Office.

James, William E. 1983. "External Shocks, Energy Policy and Macroeconomic Performance of Asian Developing Countries." In Romeo Bautista and Seiju Naya (eds.). *Energy and Structural Change in the Asia Pacific Region*. (Manila: Asian Development Bank and Philippine Institute for Development Studies.)

Krugman, P. and Taylor L. 1978. "Contractionary Effects of Devaluation." In *Journal of International Economics*, 8, pp. 445–446.

Lamberte, Mario B., Rosario G. Manasan, Erlinda M. Malanda, Josef T. Yap and Teodoro S. Untalan. 1989. "A Study of the Export Financing System in the Philippines." Working Paper Series No. 89-12, Philippine Institute for Development Studies.

Landefeld, J. Steven and James R. Hines, 1985. "National Accounting for Non-renewable Natural Resources in the Mining Industries." *Review of Income and Wealth*, Vol. 31, No. 1 (March): 1–20.

Ledesma, A. 1982. *Landless Workers and Rice Farmers: Peasant Subclasses under Agrarian Reform in the Philippines*. Los Banos, Philippines: International Rice Research Institute.

Lopez, Ramon. 1991. "Trade Policy, Economic Growth and Environmental Degradation." Paper presented at the World Bank Symposium on International Trade and the Environment, Washington, DC, Nov. 21–22.

Manasan, Rosario G. 1989. "Employment Effects of Selected Structural Adjustment Policies in the Philippines." Working Paper Series no. 89-04, Philippine Institute for Development Studies.

Manasan, Rosario G. 1990. "An Assessment of Fiscal Policy in the Philippines, 1986–1988." Working Paper Series No. 90-06, Philippine Institute for Development Studies.

Mathiesen, L. 1985. "Computational Experience in Solving Equilibrium Models by a Sequence of Linear Complementarity Problems," in *Operations Research*, (33) 6:1225–1250.

Montes, Manuel F. 1987. *Stabilization and Adjustment Policies and Programs: The Philippines*. Helsinki: World Institute for Development Economics Research of the United Nations University.

National Census and Statistics Office. *1980 Census of Population and Housing*. (Manila: National Economic and Development Agency). [Note: this publication contains the summary tables for 1948 to 1980 census.]

National Economic and Development Authority (NEDA). 1978. *The National Income Accounts: Calendar Year 1946–1975, Philippine National Income Series*. Manila: National Economic and Development Authority.

National Economic and Development Authority (NEDA). 1983. *Interindustry Accounts of the Philippines.* Manila: National Economic and Development Authority.

National Economic and Development Authority (NEDA). 1989. *Medium-Term Public Investment Program 1989–1992.* Manila: National Economic and Development Authority.

National Statistical Coordination Board (NSCB). 1990. *Philippine Statistical Yearbook 1989.* Manila: National Statistical Coordination Board.

Neri, Purita F. and Gilbert M. Llanto. 1985. "Agricultural Credit Subsidy." In *CB Review,* Oct., Manila: Central Bank of the Philippines, Vol. 37, pp. 8–16, October.

Nguiangain, Titus. 1986. *Trends and Patterns of Internal Migration in the Philippines: 1970–1980.* University of the Philippines School of Economics Discussion Paper No. 86-06.

Palanca, E. and B. Balagot-Gan. 1990. "The Urban Environment." In M.S. Delos Angeles et al. *Economic Policies and Sustainable Development,* a report submitted to the Philippine Institute for Development Studies and the Asian Development Bank.

Pante, Filologo and Erlinda Medalla. 1990. "The Philippine Industrial Sector: Policies, Programs, and Performance." Philippine Institute for Development Studies Working Paper No. 90-18.

Pauly, D. 1989. "Fisheries Resources Management in Southeast Asia: Why Bother?" In T.-E. Chau and D. Pauly (eds.) *Coastal Area Management in Southeast Asia: Policies, Management Strategies and Case Studies.* Manila: International Center for Living Aquatic Resources Management.

Power, J. 1983. "Response to Balance of Payments Crisis in the 1970s: Korea and the Philippines." Staff Paper Series No. 83-05, Philippine Institute for Development Studies.

Quisumbing, A. and C.J. Cruz. 1986. "Rural Poverty and Poverty Programs in the Philippines." In C. David et al., *Agenda for Action for the Philippines Rural Sector.* Manila: University of the Philippines and Philippine Institute for Development Studies.

Reisen, Helmut and Axel von Trotsenburg. 1988. *Developing Country Debt: The Budgetary and Transfer Problem.* Paris: Organization for Economic Cooperation and Development.

Remolona, Eli M., Mahar Mangahas, and Filologo Pante, Jr. 1986. "Foreign Debt, Balance of Payments, and the Economic Crisis of the Philippines in 1983–84." In *World Development,* Vol. 14, No. 8, August, pp. 993–1018.

Repetto, R., W. Magrath, M. Wells, C. Beer, and F. Rossini. 1989. *Wasting Assets: Natural Resources in the National Income Accounts.* Washington, DC: World Resources Institute.

Repetto, Robert. 1986. *Skimming the Water: Rent-seeking and the Performance of Public Irrigation Systems,* Washington, DC: World Resources Institute.

Reyes, Edna and Teresa Sanchez. 1990. "An Assessment of Labor and Employment Policies in the Philippines, 1986–88." Philippine Institute for Development Studies Working Paper No. 90-09.

Ribe, H. et al. 1990. "How Adjustment Programs Can Help the Poor." World Bank Discussion Paper No. 71., Washington, DC, The World Bank.

Sachs, Jeffrey D., ed. 1989. *Developing Country Debt and the World Economy.* Chicago: University of Chicago Press.

Sebastian, Iona, and Adelaida Alicbusan. 1989. "Sustainable Development: Issues in Adjustment Lending Policies." World Bank Environment Department Divisional Working Paper No. 1989-6.

Shoven, J., and J. Whalley. 1972. "A General Equilibrium Calculation of the Effects of Differential Taxation of Income from Capital in the U.S." in *Journal of Public Economics*, Vol. 1, Nos. 3–4, pp. 281–322, November.

Sicat, Gerardo P. 1986. *A Historical and Current Perspective of Philippine Economic Problems.* Manila: Philippine Institute for Development Studies.

Silvestre, Geronimo; Evangeline Niclat; and Chua Thia-Eng (eds.). 1989. *Towards Sustainable Development of the Coastal Resources of Lingaven Gulf, Philippines: Proceedings of an ASEAN/US Coastal Resources Management Project Workshop, Bauang, La Union, Philippines, 25–27 May, 1988.* Manila: International Center for Living Aquatic Resources Management.

Silvestre, Geronimo and Pauly, Daniel. 1987. "Estimate of Yield and Economic Rent from Philippine Demersal Stocks (1946–1984) Using Vessel Horsepower as an Index of Fishing Effort." In *U.P.V. Fisheries Journal* 3:1–2 pp. 11–24, (Jan–Dec).

Sosa, Mary Ann L. Celeste. 1986. "External Finance in the Economic Development of the Philippines." In *CB Review*, April, Central Bank of the Philippines. Vol. 38, pp. 28–32, April.

Strategic Study Group. 1991. *Report on the Strategic Study of the Coconut Industry 1988–89.* Manila: Joint Government-Private Sectors Steering Committee on the Coconut Industry.

Tan, Norma. 1979. "The Structure of Protection and Resource Flows in the Philippines." In Bautista, Romeo M. and John H. Power and Associates. 1979. *Industrial Promotion Policies in the Philippines.* Manila: Philippine Institute for Development Studies.

United Nations Environment Program (UNEP). 1986. *Preliminary Assessment of Land-Based Sources of Pollution in East Asian Seas.*

World Bank. 1976. *The Philippines: Prospects and Priorities for Development.* Washington, DC: World Bank.

World Bank. 1982. *Selected Issues for the 1983–87 Plan Period: Economic Report.* Washington, DC: World Bank.

World Bank. 1985. *The Philippines: Recent Trends in Poverty, Employment and Wages.* Washington, DC: World Bank.

World Bank. 1987. *Philippines: A Framework for Economic Recovery.* Washington, DC: World Bank.

World Bank. 1988a. "The Philippines—The Challenge of Poverty." Report No. 7144-PH, Washington, DC: World Bank.

World Bank. 1988b. "Philippines: Energy Sector Study." Report No. 7269-PH, Washington, DC: World Bank.

World Bank. 1989a. *World Bank Support for the Environment.* Development Committee Report No. 22, World Bank, Washington, DC: World Bank, September.

World Bank. 1989b. *Philippines: Environment and Natural Resource Management Study.* Washington, DC: World Bank.

World Bank, Country Economics Department. 1989c. *Adjustment Lending: An Evaluation of Ten Years of Experience*, Policy and Research Series No. 1, Washington, DC: World Bank.

World Resources Institute. 1990. *World Resources Report 1990–1991.* Washington, DC: World Resources Institute.

Yagci, Fahrettin, Steven Kamin and Vicki Rosenbaum. 1985. "Structural Adjustment Lending—An Evaluation of Program Design." Staff Working Paper No. 735, Washington, DC: World Bank.

World Resources Institute

1709 New York Avenue, N.W.
Washington, D.C. 20006, U.S.A.

The World Resources Institute (WRI) is a policy research center created in late 1982 to help governments, international organizations, and private business address a fundamental question: How can societies meet basic human needs and nurture economic growth without undermining the natural resources and environmental integrity on which life, economic vitality, and international security depend?

Two dominant concerns influence WRI's choice of projects and other activities:

The destructive effects of poor resource management on economic development and the alleviation of poverty in developing countries; and

The new generation of globally important environmental and resource problems that threaten the economic and environmental interests of the United States and other industrial countries and that have not been addressed with authority in their laws.

The Institute's current areas of policy research include tropical forests, biological diversity, sustainable agriculture, energy, climate change, atmospheric pollution, economic incentives for sustainable development, and resource and environmental information.

WRI's research is aimed at providing accurate information about global resources and population, identifying emerging issues, and developing politically and economically workable proposals.

In developing countries, WRI provides field services and technical program support for governments and non-governmental organizations trying to manage natural resources sustainably.

WRI's work is carried out by an interdisciplinary staff of scientists and experts augmented by a network of formal advisors, collaborators, and cooperating institutions in 50 countries.

WRI is funded by private foundations, United Nations and governmental agencies, corporations, and concerned individuals.